A COMPLETE EDITION OF
THE PAINTINGS
OF MATTHIAS GRÜNEWALD

PHAIDON

GRÜNEWALD

THE PAINTINGS

COMPLETE EDITION · WITH TWO
ESSAYS BY J.-K. HUYSMANS
AND A CATALOGUE BY E. RUHMER

EIGHTY-ONE ILLUSTRATIONS
INCLUDING SIXTEEN
IN FULL COLOUR

PHAIDON PUBLISHERS INC
DISTRIBUTED BY GARDEN CITY BOOKS
NEW YORK

LAYOUT OF THE PLATES : LUDWIG GOLDSCHEIDER

CONTENTS

J.-K. HUYSMANS
TWO ESSAYS ON GRÜNEWALD

1. *The Karlsruhe 'Crucifixion'*

CHRIST hung there, a formidable figure, on his cross, a half-trimmed branch fastened to an upright and bending like a bow under the weight of his body.

This branch seemed about to spring back and, out of sheer pity, hurl far from this world of crime and cruelty the poor body held fast by the enormous nails that transfixed the feet.

Dislocated, almost torn out of their sockets, Christ's arms looked as if they were pinioned from shoulder to wrist by the twisted cords of the muscles. The tendons of the armpit were cracking under the strain. The hands were wide open, the fingers contorted in a wild gesture in which were supplication and reproach, yet also benediction. The quivering chest was greasy with sweat. The ribs were pushed out like the staves of a barrel, and the flesh was swollen and bruised, spotted with flea-bites, speckled as with pin-pricks by splinters that had broken off from the rods at the scourging and still showed here and there under the skin.

Purulence had set in. The blood pouring over the hip from the wound in the side was thicker now and the deep red colour of mulberry juice. Rivulets of pinkish serum, of milky matter, of watery fluid the colour of grey Moselle, oozed from the chest, soaking the belly and the twisted loin-cloth below. The knees had been forced together so that the rotulae touched, while the lower legs curved apart, meeting again only where the distended feet were pressed one on top of the other. These feet had begun to putrefy and were turning green beneath the rivers of blood. Spongy and gory, they were a horrible sight, the swollen flesh rising above the head of the nail, while the clenched toes contradicted the imploring, benedictory gesture of the fingers, clawing viciously with their blue nails at the ochreous earth, impregnated with iron like the red soil of Thuringia.

Above this putrefying body the head, huge and shapeless, hung in exhaustion, a ragged crown of thorns encircling it, and an expression of pain and terror still gleaming in one haggard, half-open eye. The face was cavernous, the forehead drawn, the cheeks drained of blood; all the sunken features had a tearful look, while the mouth stretched open in a grin, the jaw contracted in atrocious tetanic spasms.

The pain had been appalling, and the death-agony so fearful that it had terrified the jeering executioners into flight.

Now, against a sky of midnight blue, the cross seemed to be bowing very low, almost level with the ground, with two figures, one on each side, watching over Christ. One was the Virgin, wearing a pale crimson hood that fell in close folds over a flowing robe of faded blue. She held herself rigid, her face pallid and swollen with weeping, staring fixedly ahead, sobbing and burying her nails in the palms of her hands. The other figure was St. John, something of a gipsy to look at or a sunburnt Swabian peasant, a big man with a beard frizzled in tight curls, clad in wide-skirted garments that looked like strips of bark: a scarlet robe and a buff-coloured cloak, the lining of which showed the feverish green of unripe lemons where it was turned back at the sleeves. Worn out with weeping, but made of sterner stuff than Mary, who was still erect but broken and exhausted, he had joined his hands in an access of emotion and was straining towards the corpse, gazing at it with his misty red eyes while a low, smothered sob choked his aching throat.

It was indeed a far cry from the debonair Golgothas adopted by the Church ever since the Renaissance to this blood-spattered, tear-stained Calvary! This tetanic Christ was not the Christ of the Rich, the Adonis of Galilee, the healthy young fop, the handsome boy with the ruddy locks, forked beard and insipid equine features, whom the faithful have worshipped for the past four hundred years. This was the Christ of St. Justin, St. Basil, St. Cyril and Tertullian, the Christ of the Early Church, a Christ who looked vulgar and ugly because he took upon himself all the sins of the world and assumed, in his humility, the most abject of appearances.

This was the Christ of the Poor, a Christ who had become flesh in the likeness of the most wretched of those he had come to redeem, the ill-favoured and the indigent, all those in fact upon whose ugliness or poverty mankind wreaks its cowardly spite. This was also the most human of Christs, a Christ frail of flesh, forsaken by the Father until such time as no further torments were possible, a Christ succoured only by his Mother, to whom he must have cried out, as do all who suffer, like a child, though by then she was powerless to help him.

By what was doubtless a supreme act of humility, he had willed that the Passion should not exceed the limits imposed by the human senses; and, in obedience to incomprehensible laws, he had consented that his Divinity should be suspended, as it were, from the first blows and insults, through the spitting and the scourging, till the unspeakable torments of

8

an interminable death-agony. In this way he had been the better able to suffer, to agonize, to die like a common thief, like a dog, basely, vilely, enduring this degradation to the bitter end, even to the ultimate horror of putrefaction, the final ignominy of decay.

Never before had realism attempted such a subject; never before had a painter explored the divine charnel-house so thoroughly, or dipped his brush so brutally in running sores and bleeding wounds. It was outrageous and it was horrifying. Grünewald was the most daring of realists, without a doubt; but as one gazed upon this Redeemer of the doss-house, this God of the morgue, there was wrought a change. Gleams of light filtered from the ulcerous head; a superhuman radiance illumined the gangrened flesh and the tortured features. This carrion spread-eagled on the cross was the tabernacle of a God; and here, his head adorned with no aureole or nimbus but a tangled crown of thorns beaded with drops of blood, Jesus appeared in his celestial supra-essence, between the Virgin, grief-stricken and blinded with tears, and St. John, whose burning eyes could find no more tears to shed.

These faces, at first sight so commonplace, shone with the ecstasy of souls transfigured by suffering. This was no common criminal, nor this a poor beggar-woman, nor this a country yokel: these were supra-terrestrial beings in the presence of a God.

Grünewald was the most daring of idealists. Never had painter so magnificently scaled the mystical heights, or so courageously leapt from the topmost peak of the spirit up into the very sphere of the heavens. He had gone to both extremes; and from the depths of squalor he had extracted the finest cordial of charity and the bitterest tears of woe. In this picture was revealed the masterpiece and supreme achievement of an art which had been bidden to represent both the invisible and the tangible, to manifest the piteous uncleanness of the body, and to sublimate the infinite distress of the soul.

(From *Là-bas*, translated by Robert Baldick.)

9

2. *The Grünewalds in the Colmar Museum*

MATTHIAS GRÜNEWALD, the painter of the Cassel *Crucifixion* which I described in *Là-bas* and which is now in the Karlsruhe Museum, has fascinated me for many years. Whence did he come, what was his life, where and how did he die? Nobody knows for certain; his very name has been disputed, and the relevant documents are lacking; the pictures now accepted as his work were formerly attributed in turn to Albrecht Dürer, Martin Schongauer and Hans Baldung Grien, while others which he never painted are conceded to him by countless handbooks and museum catalogues. . .

It is not to Mainz, Aschaffenburg, Eisenach, or even to Isenheim, whose monastery is dead, that we must go to find Grünewald's works, but to Colmar, where the master displays his genius in a magnificent ensemble, a polyptych composed of nine pieces.

There, in the old Unterlinden convent, he seizes on you the moment you go in and promptly strikes you dumb with the fearsome nightmare of a *Calvary*. It is as if a typhoon of art had been let loose and was sweeping you away, and you need a few minutes to recover from the impact, to surmount the impression of awful horror made by the huge crucified Christ dominating the nave of this museum, which is installed in the old disaffected chapel of the convent.

The scene is arranged as follows:

In the centre of the picture a gigantic Christ, of disproportionate size if compared with the figures grouped around him, is nailed to a cross which has been roughly trimmed so that patches of bare wood are exposed here and there; the transverse branch, dragged down by the hands, is bent as in the Karlsruhe *Crucifixion* into the shape of a bow. The body looks much the same in the two works: pale and shiny, dotted with spots of blood, and bristling like a chestnut-burr with splinters that the rods have left in the wounds; at the ends of the unnaturally long arms the hands twist convulsively and claw the air; the knees are turned in so that the bulbous knee-caps almost touch; while the feet, nailed one on top of the other, are just a jumbled heap of muscles underneath rotting, discoloured flesh and blue toe-nails; as for the head, it lolls on the bulging, sack-like chest patterned with stripes by the cage of the ribs. This crucified Christ would be a faithful replica of the one at Karlsruhe if the facial expression were not entirely different. Here, in fact, Jesus no longer wears the fearful rictus of tetanus; the jaw is no longer contracted, but hangs loosely, with open mouth and slavering lips.

10

Christ is less frightening here, but more humanly vulgar, more obviously dead. In the Karlsruhe panel the terrifying effect of the trismus, of the strident laugh, served to conceal the brutishness of the features, now accentuated by this imbecile slackness of the mouth. The Man-God of Colmar is nothing but a common thief who has met his end on the gallows.

That is not the only difference to be noted between the two works, for here the grouping of the figures is also dissimilar. At Karlsruhe the Virgin stands, as usual, on one side of the cross and St. John on the other; at Colmar the traditional arrangement is flouted, and the astonishing visionary that was Grünewald asserts himself, at once ingenious and ingenuous, a barbarian and a theologian, unique among religious painters.

On the right of the cross there are three figures: the Virgin, St. John and Magdalen. St. John, looking rather like an old German student with his peaky, clean-shaven face and his fair hair falling in long, dry wisps over a red robe, is holding in his arms a quite extraordinary Virgin, clad and coifed in white, who has fallen into a swoon, her face white as a sheet, her eyes shut, her lips parted to reveal her teeth. Her features are fine and delicate, and entirely modern; if it were not for the dark green dress which can be glimpsed close to the tightly clenched hands, you might take her for a dead nun; she is pitiable and charming, young and beautiful. Kneeling in front of her is a little woman who is leaning back with her hands clasped together and raised towards Christ. This oldish, fair-haired creature, wearing a pink dress with a myrtle-green lining, her face cut in half below the eyes by a veil on a level with the nose, is Magdalen. She is ugly and ungainly, but so obviously inconsolable that she grips your heart and moves it to compassion.

On the other side of the picture, to the left of the cross, there stands a tall, strange figure with a shock of sandy hair cut straight across the fore-head, limpid eyes, a shaggy beard, and bare arms, legs and feet, holding an open book in one hand and pointing to Christ with the other.

This tough old soldier from Franconia, with his camel-hair fleece showing under a loosely draped cloak and a belt tied in a big knot, is St. John the Baptist. He has risen from the dead, and in order to explain the emphatic, dogmatic gesture of the long, curling forefinger pointed at the Redeemer, the following inscription has been set beside his arm: *Illum oportet crescere, me autem minui*. 'He must increase, but I must de-crease.'

He who decreased to make way for the Messiah, who in turn died to

11

ensure the predominance of the Word in the world, is alive here, while He who was alive when he was defunct, is dead. It seems as if, in coming to life again, he is foreshadowing the triumph of the Resurrection, and that after proclaiming the Nativity before Jesus was born on earth, he is now proclaiming that Christ is born in Heaven, and heralding Easter. He has come back to bear witness to the accomplishment of the prophecies, to reveal the truth of the Scriptures; he has come back to ratify, as it were, the exactness of those words of his which will later be recorded in the Gospel of that other St. John whose place he has taken on the left of Calvary – St. John the Apostle, who does not listen to him now, who does not even see him, so engrossed is he with the Mother of Christ, as if numbed and paralysed by the manchineel of sorrow that is the cross.

So, alone in the midst of the sobbing and the awful spasms of the sacrifice, this witness of the past and the future, standing stolidly upright, neither weeps nor laments: he certifies and promulgates, impassive and resolute. And at his feet is the Lamb of the World that he baptized, carrying a cross, with a stream of blood pouring into a chalice from its wounded breast.

Thus arranged, the figures stand out against a background of gathering darkness. Behind the gibbet, which is planted on a river bank, there flows a stream of sadness, swift-moving yet the colour of stagnant water; and the somewhat theatrical presentation of the drama seems justified, so completely does it harmonize with this dismal setting, this gloom which is more than twilight but not yet night. Repelled by the sombre hues of the background, the eye inevitably turns from the glossy flesh-tints of the Redeemer, whose enormous proportions no longer hold the attention, and fastens instead upon the dazzling whiteness of the Virgin's cloak, which, seconded by the vermilion of the apostle's clothes, attracts notice at the expense of the other parts, and almost makes Mary the principal figure in the work.

That would spoil the whole picture, but the balance, about to be upset in favour of the group on the right, is maintained by the unexpected gesture of the Precursor, who in his turn seizes your attention, only to direct it towards the Son.

One might almost say that, coming to this Calvary, one goes from right to left before arriving at the centre.

This is undoubtedly what the artist intended, as is the effect produced by the disproportion between the various figures, for Grünewald is a master of pictorial equilibrium and in his other works keeps everything

12

in proportion. When he exaggerated the stature of his Christ he was trying to create a striking impression of profound suffering and great
strength; similarly he made this figure more than usually remarkable in
order to keep it in the foreground and prevent it from being completely
eclipsed by the great patch of white that is the Virgin.

As for her, it is easy to see why he gave her such prominence, easy to
understand his predilection for her – because never before had he
succeeded in painting a Madonna of such divine loveliness, such superhuman sorrow. Indeed, it is astonishing that she should appear at all in
the rebarbative work of this artist, so completely does she differ from the
type of individual he has chosen to represent God and his saints.

His Jesus is a thief, his St. John a social outcast, his Precursor a common
soldier. Even assuming that they are nothing more than German peasants,
she is obviously of very different extraction; she is a queen who has taken
the veil, a marvellous orchid growing among weeds.

Anyone who has seen both pictures – the one at Karlsruhe and the
one at Colmar – will agree that there is a clear distinction between them.
The Karlsruhe *Calvary* is better balanced and there is no danger of one's
attention wandering from the principal subject. It is also less trivial, more
awe-inspiring. You have only to compare the hideous rictus of its Christ
and the possibly more plebeian but certainly less degraded face of its St.
John with the coma of the Colmar Christ and the world-weary grimace
of the disciple for the Karlsruhe panel to appear less conjectural, more
penetrating, more effective, and, in its apparent simplicity, more powerful; on the other hand, it lacks the exquisite white Virgin and it is more
conventional, less novel and unexpected. The Colmar *Crucifixion* intro-
duces a new element into a scene treated in the same stereotyped fashion
by every other painter; it dispenses with the old moulds and discards the
traditional patterns. On reflexion, it seems to be the more imposing and
profound of the two works, but it must be admitted that introducing the
Precursor into the tragedy of Golgotha is more the idea of a theologian
and a mystic than of an artist; here it is quite likely that there was some
sort of collaboration between the painter and the purchaser, a commission
described in the minutest detail by Guido Guersi, the Abbot of Isenheim,
in whose chapel this picture was placed.

That, incidentally, was still the normal procedure long after the Middle
Ages. All the archives of the period show that when contracting with
image-carvers and painters – who regarded themselves as nothing more
than craftsmen – the bishops or monks used to draw a plan of the pro-
posed work, often even indicating the number of figures to be included

13

and explaining their significance; there was accordingly only limited scope for the artist's own initiative, as he had to work to order within strictly defined bounds.

But to return to the picture, it takes up the whole of two wood panels which, in closing, cut one of Christ's arms in two, and, when closed, bring the two groups together.

The back of the picture (for it has two faces on either side) has a separate scene on each panel: a *Resurrection* on one and an *Annunciation* on the other. Let me say straight away that the latter is bad, so that we can have done with it.

The scene is an oratory, where a book painted with deceptive realism lies open to reveal the prophecy of Isaiah, whose distorted figure, topped with a turban, is floating about in a corner of the picture, near the ceiling; on her knees in front of the book we see a fair-haired, puffy-faced woman, with a complexion reddened by the cooking-stove, pouting somewhat peevishly at a great lout with a no less ruddy complexion who is point-ing two extremely long fingers at her in a truly comical attitude of reproach. It must be admitted that the Precursor's solemn gesture in the *Crucifixion* is utterly ridiculous in this unhappy imitation, where the two fingers are extended in what looks like insolent derision. As for the curly-wigged fellow himself, with that coarse, fat, red face you would take him for a grocer rather than an angel, if it were not for the sceptre he is holding in one hand and the green-and-red wings stuck to his back. And one can but wonder how the artist who created the little white Virgin could possibly represent Our Lord's Mother in the guise of this disagree-able slut with a smirk on her swollen lips, all rigged up in her Sunday best, a rich green dress set off by a bright vermilion lining.

But if this wing leaves you with a rather painful impression, the other one sends you into raptures, for it is a truly magnificent work – unique, I would say, among the world's paintings. In it Grünewald shows him-self to be the boldest painter who has ever lived, the first artist who has tried to convey, through the wretched colours of this earth, a vision of the Godhead in abeyance on the cross and then renewed, visible to the naked eye, on rising from the tomb. With him we are, mystically speak-ing, in at the death, contemplating an art with its back to the wall and forced further into the beyond, this time, than any theologian could have instructed the artist to go. The scene is as follows:

As the sepulchre opens, some drunks in helmet and armour are knocked head over heels to lie sprawling in the foreground, sword in hand; one of them turns a somersault further off, behind the tomb, and

14

lands on his head, while Christ surges upwards, stretching out his arms and displaying the bloody commas on his hands.

This is a strong and handsome Christ, fair-haired and brown-eyed, with nothing in common with the Goliath whom we watched decomposing a moment ago, fastened by nails to the still green wood of a gibbet. All round this soaring body are rays emanating from it which have begun to blur its outline; already the contours of the face are fluctuating, the features hazing over, the hair dissolving into a halo of melting gold. The light spreads out in immense curves ranging from bright yellow to purple, and finally shading off little by little into a pale blue which in turn merges with the dark blue of the night.

We witness here the revival of a Godhead ablaze with life: the formation of a glorified body gradually escaping from the carnal shell, which is disappearing in an apotheosis of flames of which it is itself the source and seat.

Christ, completely transfigured, rises aloft in smiling majesty; and one is tempted to regard the enormous halo which encircles him, shining brilliantly in the starry night like that star of the Magi in whose smaller orb Grünewald's contemporaries used to place the infant Jesus when painting the Bethlehem story – one is tempted to regard this halo as the morning star returning, like the Precursor in the *Crucifixion*, at night: as the Christmas star grown larger since its birth in the sky, like the Messiah's body since his Nativity on earth.

Having dared to attempt this *tour de force*, Grünewald has carried it out with wonderful skill. In clothing the Saviour he has tried to render the changing colours of the fabrics as they are volatilized with Christ. Thus the scarlet robe turns a bright yellow, the closer it gets to the light-source of the head and neck, while the material grows lighter, becoming almost diaphanous in this river of gold. As for the white shroud which Jesus is carrying off with him, it reminds one of those Japanese fabrics which by subtle gradations change from one colour to another, for as it rises it takes on a lilac tint first of all, then becomes pure violet, and finally, like the last blue circle of the nimbus, merges into the indigo-black of the night.

The triumphant nature of this ascension is admirably conveyed. For once the apparently meaningless phrase 'the contemplative life of painting' takes on a meaning, for with Grünewald we enter into the domain of the most exalted mysticism and glimpse, through the simulacra of colour and line, the well-nigh tangible emergence of the Godhead from its physical shell.

15

It is here, rather than in his horrific *Calvaries*, that the undeniable originality of this prodigious artist is to be seen.

This *Crucifixion* and this *Resurrection* are obviously the Colmar Museum's brightest jewels, but the amazing colourist that was Grünewald did not exhaust the resources of his art with these two pictures; we shall find more of his work, this time stranger yet less exalted, in another double-faced diptych which also stands in the middle of the old nave.

It depicts, on one side the Nativity and a concert of angels, on the other a visit from the Patriarch of the Cenobites to St. Paul the Hermit, and the temptation of St. Anthony.

In point of fact, this *Nativity*, which is rather an exaltation of the divine Motherhood, is one with the concert of angels, as is shown by the utensils, which overlap from one wing to the other and are cut in two when the panels are brought together.

The subject of this dual painting is admittedly obscure. In the left-hand wing the Virgin is seen against a distant, bluish landscape dominated by a monastery on a hill – doubtless Isenheim Abbey; on her left, beside a crib, a tub and a pot, a fig-tree is growing, and a rose-tree on her right. Fair-haired, with a florid complexion, thick lips, a high, bare brow and a straight nose, she is wearing a blue cloak over a carmine-coloured dress. She is not the servant-girl type, and has not come straight from the sheep-pen like her sister in the *Annunciation*, but for all that she is still just an honest German woman bred on beer and sausages: a farmer's wife, if you like, with servant-girls under her who look like the Mary of that other picture, but nothing more. As for the Child, who is very lifelike and very skilfully portrayed, he is a sturdy little Swabian peasant, with a snub nose, sharp eyes, and a pink, smiling face. And finally, in the sky above Jesus and Mary and below God the Father, who is smothered in clouds of orange and gold, swarms of angels are whirling about like scattered petals caught in a shower of saffron sunbeams.

All these figures are completely earthbound, and the artist seems to have realized this, for there is a radiance emanating from the Child's head and lighting up the Mother's fingers and face. Grünewald obviously wanted to convey the idea of divinity by means of these gleams of light filtering through the flesh, but this time he was not bold enough to achieve the desired effect: the luminous glow fails to conceal either the vulgarity of the face or the coarseness of the features.

So far, in any event, the subject is clear enough, but the same cannot be said of the complementary scene on the right-hand wing.

Here, in an ultra-Gothic chapel, with gold-scumbled pinnacles bristling with sinuous statues of prophets nestling among chicory, hop, knapweed and holly leaves, on top of slender pillars entwined by plants with singularly jagged leaves and twisted stems, are angels of every description, some in human form and others appearing simply as heads fitted into haloes shaped like funeral wreaths or collarettes: angels with pink or blue faces, angels with multicoloured or monochrome wings, angels playing the angelot or the theorbo or the viola d'amore, and all of them, like the pasty-faced, unhealthy-looking one in the foreground, gazing in adoration at the great Virgin in the other wing.

The effect is decidedly odd, but even odder is the appearance, beside these pure spirits and between two of the slender columns in the chapel, of another, smaller Virgin, this time crowned with a diadem of red-hot iron, who, her face suffused with a golden halo, her eyes cast down and her hands joined in prayer, is kneeling before the other Virgin and the Child.

What is the significance of this strange creature, who evokes the same weird impression as the girl with the cock and the money-pouch in Rembrandt's *Night Watch* – a girl likewise nimbed with a gentle radiance? Is this phantom queen a diminutive St. Anne or some other saint? She looks just like a Madonna, and a Madonna is what she must be. In painting her Grünewald has clearly tried to reproduce the light effect which blurs the features of Christ in his *Resurrection*, but it is difficult to see why he should do so here. It may be, of course, that he wanted to represent the Virgin, crowned after her Assumption, returning to earth with her angelic retinue to pay homage to that Motherhood which was her supreme glory; or, on the other hand, she may still be in this world, foreseeing the celebration of her triumph after her painful life among us. But this last hypothesis is promptly demolished by Mary's unheeding attitude, for she appears to be completely unaware of the presence of the winged musicians, and intent only on amusing the Child. In fact, these are all unsupported theories, and it would be simpler to admit that we just do not understand. I need only add that these two pictures are painted in loud colours which are sometimes positively shrill to make it clear that this faery spectacle presented in a crazy Gothic setting leaves one feeling vaguely uncomfortable.

As a refreshing contrast, however, one can always linger in front of the panel showing St. Anthony talking with St. Paul; it is the only restful picture in the whole series, and one is already so accustomed to the vehemence of the others that one is almost tempted to find it too unexciting, to consider it too anodyne.

In a rural setting that is all bright blue and moss green, the two recluses are sitting face to face: St. Anthony curiously attired, for a man who has just crossed the desert, in a pearl-grey cloak, a blue robe and a pink cap; St. Paul dressed in his famous robe of palms, which has here become a mere robe of rushes, with a doe at his feet and the traditional raven flying through the trees to bring him the usual hermit's meal of a loaf of bread.

In this picture the colouring is quiet and delicate, the composition superb: the subject may have put a certain restraint upon Grünewald, but he has lost none of the qualities which make him a great painter. To anyone who prefers the cordial, expected welcome of a pleasing picture to the uncertainties of a visit to some more turbulent work of art, this wing will undoubtedly seem the nicest, soundest and sanest of them all. It constitutes a halt in the man's mad gallop – but only a brief halt, for he sets off again almost at once, and in the next wing we find him giving free rein to his fancy, caracolling along dangerous paths, and sounding a full fanfare of colours – as violent and tempestuous as he was in his other works.

The Temptation of St. Anthony must have given him enormous pleasure, for this picture of a demons' sabbath waging war on the good monk called for the most convulsive attitudes, the most extravagant forms and the most vehement colours. Nor was he slow to grasp this opportunity of exploiting the droller side of the supernatural. But if there is extra-ordinary life and colour in the *Temptation*, there is also utter confusion. Indeed, the picture is in such a tangle that it is impossible to distinguish between the limbs of the various devils, and one would be hard put to it to say which paw or wing beating or scratching the Saint belonged to which animal or bird.

The frantic hurly-burly in which these creatures are taking part is none the less captivating for that. It is true that Grünewald cannot match the ingenious variety and the very orderly disorder of a Bruegel or a Hierony-mus Bosch, and that there is nothing here to compare with the diversity of clearly delineated and discreetly insane larvae which you find in the *Fall of the Angels* in the Brussels Museum: our painter has a more restricted fancy, a more limited imagination. He gives us a few demons' heads stuck with stags' antlers or straight horns, a shark's maw, and what appears to be the muzzle of a walrus or a calf; the rest of his super-numeraries all belong to the bird family, and with arms in place of feet look like the offspring of empuses that have been covered by angry cocks.

All these escapees from an infernal aviary are clustered excitedly around the anchorite, who has been thrown on his back and is being dragged

18

along by his hair. Looking rather like a Dutch version of Father Becker with his flowing beard, St. Anthony is screaming with fear, trying to protect his face with one hand, and in the other clutching his stick and his rosary, which are being pecked at furiously by a hen wearing a carapace in lieu of feathers. The monstrous creatures are all closing in for the kill; a sort of giant parrot, with a green head, crimson arms, yellow claws and grey-gold plumage, is on the point of clubbing the monk, while another demon is pulling off his grey cloak and chewing it up, and yet others are joining in, swinging rib-bones and frantically tearing his clothes to get at him.

Considered simply as a man, St. Anthony is wonderfully lifelike in gesture and expression; and once you have taken your fill of the whole dizzy scramble, you may notice two thought-provoking details which you overlooked at first, hidden as they seem to be in the bottom corners. One, in the right-hand corner, is a sheet of paper on which a few lines are written; the other is a weird, hooded creature, sitting quite naked beside the Saint, and writhing in agony.

The paper bears this inscription: *Ubi eras Jhesu bone, ubi eras, quare non affuisti ut sanares vulnera mea?* – which can be translated as: 'Where were you, good Jesus, where were you? And why did you not come and dress my wounds?'

This plaint, doubtless uttered by the hermit in his distress, is heard and answered, for if you look right at the top of the picture you will see a legion of angels coming down to release the captive and overpower the demons.

It may be asked whether this desperate appeal is not also being made by the monster lying in the opposite corner of the picture and raising his weary head heavenwards. And is this creature a larva or a man? Whatever it may be, one thing is certain: no painter has ever gone so far in the representation of putrefaction, nor does any medical textbook contain a more frightening illustration of skin disease. This bloated body, moulded in greasy white soap mottled with blue, and mamillated with boils and carbuncles, is the hosanna of gangrene, the song of triumph of decay!

Was Grünewald's intention to depict a demon in its most despicable form? I think not. On careful examination the figure in question is seen to be a decomposing, suffering human being. And if it is recalled that this picture, like the others, comes from the Anthonite Abbey of Isenheim, everything becomes clear. A brief account of the aims of this Order will, I think, suffice to explain the riddle.

The Anthonite or Anthonine Order was founded in the Dauphiné in 1093 by a nobleman called Gaston whose son was cured of the burning sickness through the intercession of St. Anthony; its *raison d'être* was the care of people suffering from this type of disease. Placed under the Rule of St. Augustine, the Order spread rapidly across France and Germany, and became so popular in the latter country that during Grünewald's lifetime, in 1502, the Emperor Maximilian I granted it, as a mark of esteem, the right to bear the Imperial arms on its escutcheon, together with the blue tau which the monks themselves were to wear on their black habit.

Now there was at that time an Anthonite abbey at Isenheim which had already stood there for over a century. The burning sickness was still rife, so that the monastery was in fact a hospital. We know too that it was the Abbot of Isenheim, or rather, to use the terminology of this Order, the Preceptor, Guido Guersi, who commissioned this polyptych from Grünewald.

It is now easy to understand the inclusion of St. Anthony in this series of paintings. It is also easy to understand the terrifying realism and meticulous accuracy of Grünewald's Christ-figures, which he obviously modelled on the corpses in the hospital mortuary; the proof is that Dr. Richet, examining his *Crucifixions* from the medical point of view, states that 'attention to detail is carried to the point of indicating the inflammatory halo which develops around minor wounds'. Above all, it is easy to understand the picture – painted from life in the hospital ward – of that hideous, agonized figure in the *Temptation*, which is neither a larva nor a demon, but simply a poor wretch suffering from the burning sickness.

It should be added that the written descriptions of this scourge which have come down to us correspond in every respect with Grünewald's pictorial description, so that any doctor who wants to know what form this happily extinct disease took can go and study the sores and the affected tissues shown in the painting at Colmar.*

The burning sickness, also known as holy fire, hell fire and St. Anthony's fire, first appeared in Europe in the tenth century, and swept the whole continent. It partook of both gangrenous ergotism and the plague, showing itself in the form of apostems and abscesses, gradually spreading to the arms and legs, and after burning them up, detaching them little by little from the torso. That at least is how it was described in

---

*Two doctors have given their attention to this figure: Charcot and Richet. The former, in *Les Syphilitiques dans l'art*, sees it above all as a picture of the so-called 'Neapolitan disease'; the latter, in *L'Art et la Médecine*, hesitates between a disease of that type and leprosy.

the fifteenth century by the biographers of St. Lydwine, who was afflicted with the disease. Dom Félibien likewise mentions it in his History of Paris, where he says of the epidemic which ravaged France in the twelfth century: 'The victims' blood was affected by a poisonous inflammation which consumed the whole body, producing tumours which developed into incurable ulcers and caused thousands of deaths.'

What is certain is that not a single remedy proved successful in checking the disease, and that often it was cured only by the intercession of the Virgin and the saints.

The Virgin's intervention is still commemorated by the shrine of Notre-Dame des Ardents in Picardy, and there is a well-known cult of the holy candle of Arras. As for the saints, apart from St. Anthony, people invoked St. Martin, who had saved the lives of a number of victims gathered together in a church dedicated to him; prayers were also said to St. Israel, Canon of Le Dorat, to St. Gilbert, Bishop of Meaux, and finally to Geneviève. This was because, one day in the reign of Louis the Fat when her shrine was being carried in solemn procession around the Cathedral of Paris, she cured a crowd of people afflicted with the disease who had taken refuge in the basilica, and this miracle caused such a stir that, in order to preserve the memory of it, a church was built in the same city under the invocation of Sainte-Geneviève des Ardents; it no longer exists, but the Parisian Breviary still celebrates the Saint's feast-day under that name.

But to return to Grünewald, who, I repeat, has clearly left us a truthful picture of a victim of this type of gangrene, the Colmar Museum also contains a predella *Entombment*, with a livid Christ speckled with flecks of blood, a hard-faced St. John with pale ochre-coloured hair, a heavily veiled Virgin and a Magdalen disfigured by tears. However, this predella is merely a feeble echo of Grünewald's great Crucifixions: it would be astounding, seen on its own in a collection of canvases by other painters, but here it is not even astonishing.

Mention must be made as well of two rectangular wings: one depicting a little bandy-legged St. Sebastian larded with arrows; the other – a panel cited by Sandrart – St. Anthony holding the Tau, the crozier of his Order – a St. Anthony so solemn and so thoughtful that he can even ignore the demon busily breaking window-panes behind him. And that brings us to the end of our review of this master-painter's works. You take leave of him spellbound for ever. And if you look for his origins you will look in vain, for none of the painters who preceded him or who were his contemporaries resembles him.

One can perhaps discern a certain foreign influence in Grünewald's work; as Goutzwiller points out in his booklet on the Colmar Museum, it is possible to see a reminiscence or a vague imitation of the contemporary Italian landscape manner in the way in which he plans his settings and sprinkles his skies with blue. Had he travelled in Italy, or had he seen pictures by Italian masters in Germany – perhaps at Isenheim itself, since the Preceptor Guido Guersi, to judge by his name, hailed from beyond the Alps? No one knows; but in any event, the very existence of this influence is open to question. It is, in fact, by no means certain that this man who anticipates modern painting, reminding one sometimes of Renoir with his acid colours and of the Japanese with his skilful nuances, did not arrange his landscapes without benefit of memories or copies, painting them from nature as he found them in the countryside of Thuringia or Swabia; for he could easily have seen the bright bluish backcloth of his *Nativity* in those parts. Nor do I share Goutzwiller's opinion that there is an unmistakable 'Italian touch' in the inclusion of a cluster of palm-trees in the picture of the two anchorites. The introduction of this type of tree into an Oriental landscape is so natural and so clearly called for by the subject that it does not imply any outside suggestion or influence. In any event, if Grünewald did know the work of foreign artists, it is surprising that he should have confined himself to borrowing their method of arranging and depicting skies and woods, while refraining from copying their technique of composition and their way of painting Jesus and the Virgin, the angels and the saints.

His landscapes, I repeat, are definitely German, as is proved by certain details. These may strike many people as having been invented to create an effect, to add a note of pathos to the drama of Calvary, yet in fact they are strictly accurate. This is certainly true of the bloody soil in which the Karlsruhe cross is planted, and which is no product of the imagination. Grünewald did much of his painting in Thuringia, where the earth, saturated with iron oxide, is red; I myself have seen it sodden with rain and looking like the mud of a slaughter-house, a swamp of blood.

As for his human figures, they are all typically German, and he owes just as little to Italian art when it comes to the arrangement of dress fabrics. These he has really woven himself, and they are so distinctive that they would be sufficient in themselves to identify his pictures among those of all other painters. With him we are far removed from the little puffs, the sharp elbows and the short frills of the Primitives; he drapes his clothes magnificently in flowing movements and long folds, using materials that are closely woven and deeply dyed. In the Karlsruhe *Cruci-*

fixion they have something about them suggestive of bark ripped from a tree: the same harsh quality as the picture itself. At Colmar this impression is not so pronounced, but they still reveal the multiplicity of layers, the slight stiffness of texture, the ridges and the hollows which are the hallmark of Grünewald's work; this is particularly true of Christ's loincloth and St. John the Baptist's cloak.

Here again he is nobody's pupil, and we have no alternative but to put him down in the history of painting as an exceptional artist, a barbarian of genius who bawls out coloured prayers in an original dialect, an outlandish tongue.

His tempestuous soul goes from one extreme to another, restless and storm-tossed even during moments of deliberate repose; but just as it is deeply moving when meditating on the episodes of the Passion, so it is erratic and well-nigh baroque when reflecting on the joys of the Nativity. The truth is that it simpers and stammers when there is no torturing to be done, for Grünewald is the painter of tombs rather than cribs, and he can only depict the Virgin successfully when he makes her suffer. Otherwise he sees her as red-faced and vulgar, and there is such a difference between his Madonnas of the sorrowful mysteries and his Madonnas of the joyful mysteries that one wonders whether he was not following an aesthetic system, a scheme of intentional antitheses.

It is, indeed, quite likely that he decided that the quality of divine Motherhood would only come out clearly under the stress of the suffering endured at the foot of the cross. This theory would certainly fit in with the one he adopted whenever he wished to glorify the divine nature of the Son, for he always painted the living Christ as the Psalmist and Isaiah pictured him – as the poorest and ugliest of men – and only restored his divine appearance to him after his Passion and death. In other words, Grünewald made the ugliness of the crucified Messiah the symbol of all the sins of the world which Christ took upon himself, thus illustrating a doctrine which was expounded by Tertullian, St. Cyprian, St. Cyril, St. Justin and countless others, and which was current for a good part of the Middle Ages.

He may also have been the victim of a technique which Rembrandt was to use after him: the technique of suggesting the idea of divinity by means of the light emanating from the very face that is supposed to represent it. Admirable in his *Resurrection of Christ*, this secretion of light is less convincing when he applies it to the little Virgin in the *Angelic Concert* and completely ineffective when he uses it to portray the fundamentally vulgar Child in the *Nativity*.

23

He probably placed too much reliance on these devices, crediting them with an efficacy they could not possess. It should, indeed, be noted that, if the light spinning like an artificial sun around the risen Christ suggests to us a vision of a divine world, it is because Christ's face lends itself to that idea by its gentle beauty. It strengthens rather than weakens the significance and effect of that huge halo, which in turn softens and enhances the features, veiling them in a mist of gold.

Such is the complete Grünewald polyptych in the Colmar Museum. I do not intend to deal here with those paintings attributed to him which are scattered among other art-galleries and churches, and which for the most part are not his work. I shall also pass over the Munich *St. Erasmus and St. Maurice*, which, if it must be accepted as his work, is cold and uncharacteristic; I shall even set aside the *Fall of Jesus*, which like the famous *Crucifixion* has been transferred from Cassel to Karlsruhe, and which is undoubtedly genuine. It shows a blue-clad Christ on his knees, dragging his cross, in the midst of a group of soldiers dressed in red and executioners dressed in white with pistachio stripes. He is gritting his teeth and digging his fingernails into the wood, but his expression is less of suffering than of anger, and he looks like a damned soul. This, in short, is a bad Grünewald.

Confining myself therefore to the brilliant, awe-inspiring flower of his art, the Karlsruhe *Crucifixion* and the nine pieces at Colmar, I find that his work can only be defined by coupling together contradictory terms.

The man is, in fact, a mass of paradoxes and contrasts. This Orlando furioso of painting is forever leaping from one extravagance to another, but when necessary the frenzied demoniac turns into a highly skilled artist who is up to every trick of the trade. Though he loves nothing better than a startling clash of colours, he can also display, when in good form, an extremely delicate sense of light and shade – his *Resurrection* is proof of that – and he knows how to combine the most hostile hues by gently coaxing them together with adroit chromatic diplomacy.

He is at once naturalistic and mystical, savage and sophisticated, ingenuous and deceitful. One might say that he personifies the fierce and pettifogging spirit of the Germany of his time, a Germany excited by the ideas of the Reformation. Was he involved, like Cranach and Dürer, in that emotional religious movement which was to end in the most austere coldness of the heart, once the Protestant swamp had frozen over? I cannot say – though he certainly lacks nothing of the harsh fervour and vulgar faith which characterized the illusory springtide of the early sixteenth century. For me, however, he personifies still more the

24

religious piety of the sick and the poor. That awful Christ who hung dying over the altar of the Isenheim hospital would seem to have been made in the image of the ergotics who prayed to him; they must surely have found consolation in the thought that this God they invoked had suffered the same torments as themselves, and had become flesh in a form as repulsive as their own; and they must have felt less forsaken, less contemptible. It is easy to see why Grünewald's name, unlike the names of Holbein, Cranach and Dürer, is not to be found in the account-books or the records of commissions left by emperors and princes. His pestiferous Christ would have offended the taste of the courts; he could only be understood by the sick, the unhappy and the monks, by the suffering members of Christ.

(From *Trois Primitifs*, translated by Robert Baldick.)

SHORT BIBLIOGRAPHY

BOCK, FRANZ: *Die Werke des Matthias Grüne-wald*. Studien zur deutschen Kunstgeschichte 54, Munich 1904.

SCHMID, HEINRICH ALFRED: *Die Gemälde und Zeichnungen von Mathias Grünewald*, Straßburg 1907 (plates), 1911 (text).

JOSTEN, HANNS HEINZ: *Matthias Grünewald*. Bielefeld-Leipzig 1913, 1921.

MAYER, AUGUST L.: *Matthias Grünewald*. Munich 1919, 1920.

HAGEN, OSKAR: *Matthias Grünewald*. München 1919 (4th ed.) 1923.

RÉAU, LOUIS: *Matthias Grünewald et le Retable de Colmar*. Nancy-Paris 1920.

NIEMEYER, WILH.: *Matthias Grünewald*. Berlin 1921.

FEURSTEIN, HEINRICH: *Grünewald*, in Beiträge zur Geschichte der deutschen Kunst. Augsburg 1924.

NAUMANN, HANS HEINR.: *Das Grünewald-Problem und das neuentdeckte Selbstbildnis des 20-jährigen Mathis Nithart aus dem Jahre 1475*. Jena 1930.

FEURSTEIN, HEINRICH: *Matthias Grünewald*. Bonn 1930.

KNAPP, FRITZ: *Grünewald*. Bielefeld-Leipzig 1935.

BURKHARD, A.: *Mathias Grünewald, Personality and Accomplishment*. Cambridge (Mass.) 1936.

HÜNICKEN, ROLF: *Grünewald in Halle*. Zeitschrift für Kunstgeschichte 1936, 219 ff.

FRAENGER, WILH.: *Matthias Grünewald, ein physiognomischer Versuch*. Berlin 1936.

WIND, EDGAR: *Studies in Allegorical Portraiture I* (Albrecht von Brandenburg as St. Erasmus), in Journal of the Warburg Institute, vol. I, No. 2, October 1937, pp. 142–162.

ZÜLCH, WALTER KARL: *Der historische Grüne-wald*. Munich 1938. *Short popular edition:* Munich 1938, 1949.

HÜRLIMANN, M. – DEUSCH, W. R.: *Grünewald, Die Werke des Mathis Gothart Neithart*. Zurich 1939.

HAUG, HANS: *Grünewald* (2nd ed.) Paris 1939.

SCHOENBERGER, GUIDO: *The Drawings of Mathis Gothart Nithart, called Grünewald*. New York 1948.

SALM, CHRISTIAN ALTGRAF: *Grünewalds Flügel zum Heller-Altar*. Münchener Jahrbuch 1951, 118 ff.

WINKLER, FRIEDRICH: *Der Marburger Grüne-wald-Fund*. Zeitschrift für Kunstwissenschaft 1952, 155 ff.

STENGEL, WALTHER: *Der neue Grünewald-Fund*. Zeitschrift für Kunstwissenschaft 1952, 65 ff. (Berlin Grünewald find).

FRAUNDORFER, PAUL: *Altes und Neues zur Grünewald-Forschung*. Herbipolis Jubilans, Würz-burg 1952, 373 ff.

BEHLING, LOTTLISA: *Die Handzeichnungen des Mathis Gothart Nithart gen. Grünewald*. Weimar 1955.

ZÜLCH, WALTER KARL: *Grünewald* (including the recent finds). Leipzig 1956.

MEIER, MICHAEL: *Grünewald, Das Werk des Mathis Gothardt Neithardt*. Zürich-Freiburg i. Br. 1957.

VOGT, ADOLF MAX: *Grünewald, Meister gegen-klassischer Malerei*. Zurich-Stuttgart 1957.

MATTHIAS GRÜNEWALD

NAME: Grünewald is always referred to as 'Master Mathis' in the documents of 1501/1516. He himself also signed the drawing in the Ashmolean Museum, Oxford: '(M)athis'. Other works before 1519 bear the monogram 'M.G.', which has been deciphered as 'Mathis Gothardt'. Gothardt probably was his real surname.

In 1519, however, Grünewald signed his 'Maria-Schnee' (Our Lady of the Snows) altarpiece for the collegiate church of Aschaffenburg with the letters G in M and N above; he was using the double name Mathis Gothardt Neithardt.

After 1519 he again, to begin with, reverted to Mathis Gothardt until in 1527 he appeared in Frankfurt a.M. as Mathis Nithardt. In Halle in 1528 he was once more called Mathes Gothardt while in a posthumous document drawn up immediately afterwards in Frankfurt he is called 'Mathis Nithardt or Gothardt'.

With one exception Grünewald's adopted son Andreas Neithardt, the latter's master Arnold Rücker in Seligenstadt and his guardian Hans von Saarbrücken in Frankfurt all call the deceased artist 'Mathis Neithart'. The idea seems plausible that Neithart was the name of Andreas' mother, who brought her son with her when she married – possibly around 1519. At that time, on one occasion Grünewald added his wife's name to his own – a custom that is still practised, e.g. in Switzerland, today. Andreas is called Neithart in all the documents, but with the one exception Grünewald is only referred to as Neithart in documents which are in some way related to his son.

Joachim von Sandrart, Grünewald's first biographer (1675, 1679, 1683) did not add the name 'Grünewald' – which he got from an obscure source – to the christian name Matthaeus until his *Teutsche Academie* was in the press (this was elicited by Zülch, 1938, 5).

PLACE OF BIRTH: The artist's name is found connected with the following places: 'from Aschaffenburg' (1514, but referring to 1511), 'from' or 'in' Seligenstadt (1513, 1514, etc.). In a record of a lawsuit in Frankfurt of 1527 the artist is called 'Mathis Nithardt of Würtzburg', in a distraint suit of 1528 'Mathis de Würtzburg' (Zülch 1938, 371, 373) while Grünewald's friend, Hans of Saarbrücken, wrote the same name on the cases containing Grünewald's effects which he stored in his house 'Zum Einhorn'. Seeing that the other names refer only to places where he was living at the time or had just left, Würzburg really does seem to indicate the place of his birth.

In Würzburg, too, his parents were alleged to have been discovered in the persons of Alderman Hans Neithart, engineer and clerk of the works, who was a merchant by profession and died in 1471, and his wife Elizabeth whose maiden name was Oettinger (O. Fraundorfer, 1952, 393). There is, however, little to substantiate this hypothesis – particularly in view of the fact that until 1519 Mathis evidently called himself Gothardt and not Nithardt and also signed his earlier works as such.

DATE OF BIRTH: The year of Grünewald's birth, for which we have no certain evidence, is hotly disputed. Between 1480 and 1490 a 'master Mathis the painter' worked in Aschaffenburg and executed several, often minor works, none of which can be traced with any certainty. His name disappears from the Aschaffenburg archives after 1490; but Grünewald does not appear until 1500 and then in Seligenstadt a.M. It is extremely unlikely that the two artists are identical.

When Mathis settled in Seligenstadt in 1500 he was already free master (Fraundorfer 1952, 387). If the move to Seligenstadt and the opening of a workshop there is connected with his acquired master title then, following the general custom, we may assume that in 1500 Mathis was about 25 or 30 years old, that is to say he was born between 1470/75. This conclusion is supported in particular by the evidence of his artistic style. An artist who painted the Munich *Mocking of Christ* in 1503 and during the following 25 years evolved along the lines revealed in his subsequent, mostly datable, paintings, can have had no considerable late-Gothic past, such as would have to be assumed if he had been born as early as 1455 (Naumann 1930, 7) and were to be identified with master Mathis active at Aschaffenburg between 1480 and 1490. Grünewald was never late-Gothic in the sense of, say, Hans Holbein the elder or Tilman Riemenschneider, b. *c.* 1460, but from his first known painting worked in the mannerist-painterly style that also characterizes the work of painters such as Jörg Ratgeb (b. *c.* 1480), Albrecht Altdørfer (*c.* 1480), Nikolaus Manuel Deutsch (1484), Hans Baldung-Grien (*c.* 1485) and sculptors such as Hans Leinberger (b. *c.* 1480/85). If we accept him as the most representative personality and innovator of this style, the so-called 'Danube-School', named, but much too narrowly, from the geographical area of its greatest concentration, then he may be a little older than these lesser masters and, like his great contemporary and counterpart Albrecht Dürer, born about 1470; like Dürer too, he died in 1528.

BIOGRAPHY: After settling in Seligenstadt – a little town on the Main which enjoyed many privileges but had no kind of artistic life – buying a house there in 1500/01 and taking a second one in 1502, he opened a workshop for carvers and painters which flourished until at least 1526. From about 1508 Seligenstadt could record a greater influx of artists. In 1509 Grünewald owned a new house and leased a brook that flowed into the river Main near a mill, where soon after he also owned a pond.

About this time, as we learn from a document of 1515, he must already have been 'servant', that is court painter, to Uriel Gemmingen, archbishop of Mainz, who remained in office from 1508 until 1514. Around 1511 as the prince's leading art official he was 'supervisor or clerk of the works' for the rebuilding of the Aschaffenburg palace. After the death of Uriel in 1514 Albrecht of Hohenzollern became reigning prince. At the end of August 1516 – evidently after a temporary resignation from court-service – Mathis claimed the payment of his salary in Mainz. His last works prove that he really was in Albrecht's service, at least two

28

were certainly made for the cardinal. A brevet and elegant court dresses are listed in 1528 in Frankfurt in the inventory of Grünewald's estate (Zülch 1938, 373 f.). The servant and court painter Grünewald must also have been supervisor or clerk of the works for cardinal Albrecht's new buildings in Halle. Mathis was absent from Seligenstadt between 1520/23 and as this is the time when Albrecht's collegiate church was being built in Halle, for which Mathis painted at least two altarpieces, he was probably there at the time. His employment at the court, however, did not prevent him from serving other patrons. First among these is the Aschaffenburg canon Heinrich Reitzmann, for whom Grünewald painted altarpieces and epitaphs in 1504, 1511(?), 1514 and 1517/19. His greatest work, the Isenheim altarpiece, which bears the date 1515, was commissioned by Guido Guersi, the preceptor of the Antonite monastery of Isenheim (Alsace). As hydraulic engineer Grünewald was frequently called to give expert opinions on fountains, e.g. in 1510 at Bingen a. Rhein and in 1517 at Aschaffenburg.

The fact that Grünewald received his last instalment from the court exchequer on 27 Feb. 1526 and shortly after left the electorate of Mainz led to the former assumption that like many another artist he had participated in the peasant rising of 1525. Court officials who took part in the disturbances were dismissed by the cardinal in 1526. In Grünewald's Frankfurt estate were found in 1528 a document (guaranty) referring to the 'revolt', a New Testament, 'much Lutheran trash', an explanation of the 12 articles of the Christian Faith (the so-called peasant articles?) and 27 sermons of Luther the possession of which was a punishable offence (Zülch 1938, 373–375). Before leaving Seligenstadt Grünewald apprenticed his adopted son Andreas to the carver and cabinet-maker Arnold Rücker of Berlin.

Grünewald moved to Frankfurt, where he stayed until the early summer of 1527 in the house 'zum Einhorn' belonging to the silk embroiderer Hans von Saarbrücken (but according to Fraundorfer's recent research he was still recorded as owning property in Seligenstadt). According to Zülch, Mathis occupied himself with the preparation and sale of a medical drug and the sale of colours and also did technical drawings. Here, too, he drew up his (lost) will in 1527.

Grünewald left Frankfurt in the summer and moved to Halle, where he was given a job as hydraulic engineer, not at the court but by the town magistrate who had Protestant leanings, although, in the words of his two death witnesses, he did not 'achieve much' in this office. Grünewald died at the end of August 1528 in the house of one of his Halle friends, perhaps the silk embroiderer Hans Plock, who owned drawings by the artist and worked from his designs. Apparently he left some debts.

According to Sandrart (1675) Grünewald 'lived a solitary and melancholy life and was unhappily married'. The marriage does not seem to have taken place until Grünewald was well advanced in years; his wife brought a son Andreas with her who was adopted by Grünewald (Zülch 1956, 30). We hear of Andreas for the last time in 1553 when he receives permission to teach in a school in Frankfurt.

E. RUHMER

PLATES

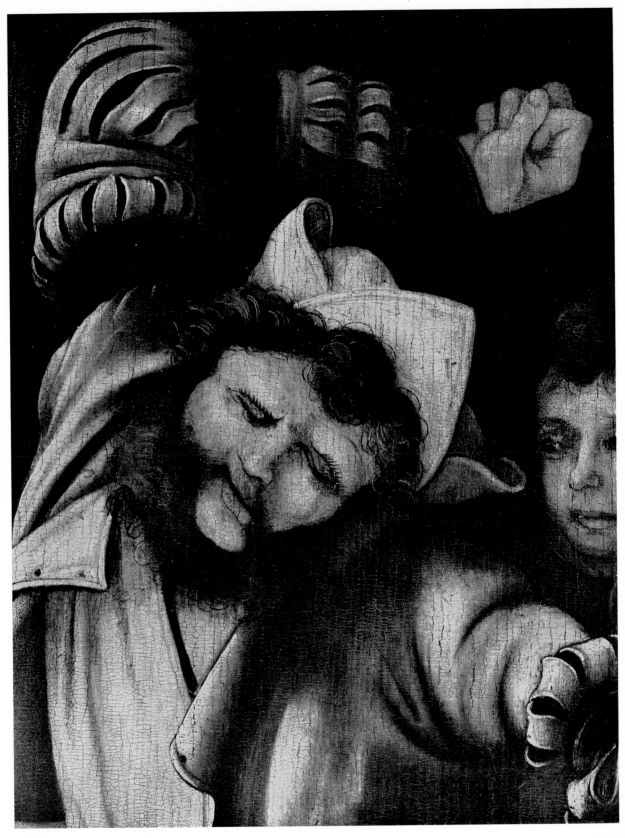

3. *Soldier*. Detail from Plate 1

S · LAVRENCIVS · M·N

4. *Saint Lawrence*. 1511–1512.
Frankfurt, Staedel Institute

S · CIRIÆCVS ·

5. *Saint Cyriac.* 1511–1512.
Frankfurt, Staedel Institute

6. *Saint Elizabeth.* 1511–1512.
Donaueschingen, Fürstenbergische Galer

7. *Saint Lucy* (?). 1511–1512.
Donaueschingen, Fürstenbergische Galerie

8. *Saint Cyriac*. Detail from Plate 5

9. *Saint Lucy* (?). Detail from Plate 7

10. *Hand of Saint Lawrence*. Detail from Plate 4

11. *Hand of Saint Lucy* (?). Detail from Plate 7

12. *Christ on the Cross with the Three Maries, John and Longinus.* Before 1515. Basel, Öffentliche Kunstsammlung

13. *Saint John the Evangelist and Longinus.* Detail from Plate 12

A

B

C

D

14–15. *The Isenheim Altarpiece.* About 1513–1515.
Originally on the high altar of the church of the Antonite monastery at Isenheim,
now in the Unterlinden Museum at Colmar (Alsace)

A. First stage: *Saint Anthony – Crucifixion – Saint Sebastian – Entombment*

B. Second stage: *Annunciation – Christmas picture – Resurrection*

C. Third stage: *The two Hermits* – Carved centrepiece (attributed to Niklas Hagnower) –
Temptation of Saint Anthony – carved predella (by Desiderius Beychel)

D. Predella: *Entombment with the Virgin, Saint John and Mary Magdalen*

16–17. *Christ on the Cross with the Virgin, Saint John the Evangelist, Magdalen and Saint John the Bapti*

Dated 1515. Centre panel of the first stage of the Isenheim altarpiece (Plate 14–A)

18. *The Virgin and Saint John the Evangelist.* Detail from Plate 16

19. *Mary Magdalen*. Detail from Plate 16

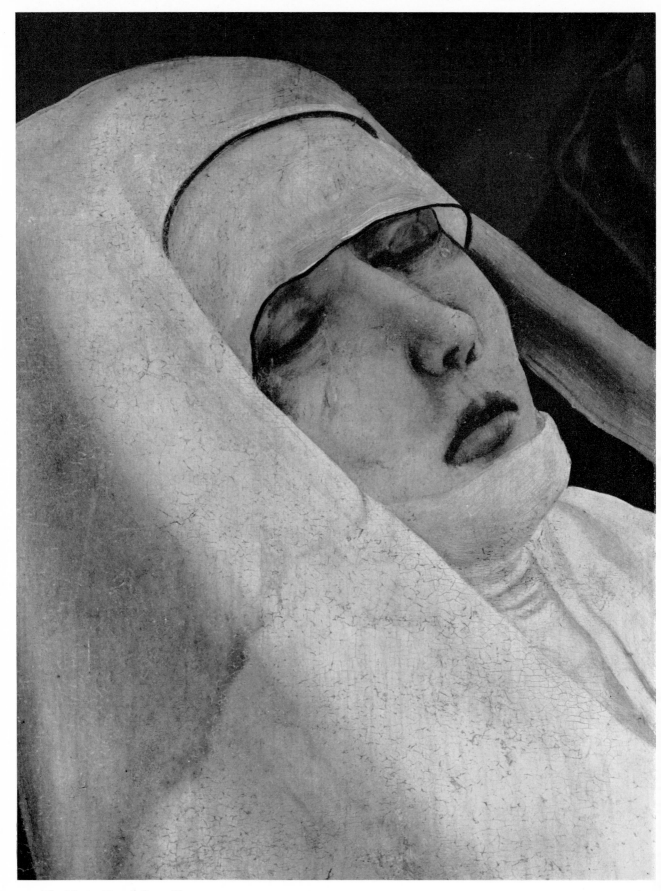

20. *The Virgin*. Detail from Plate 16

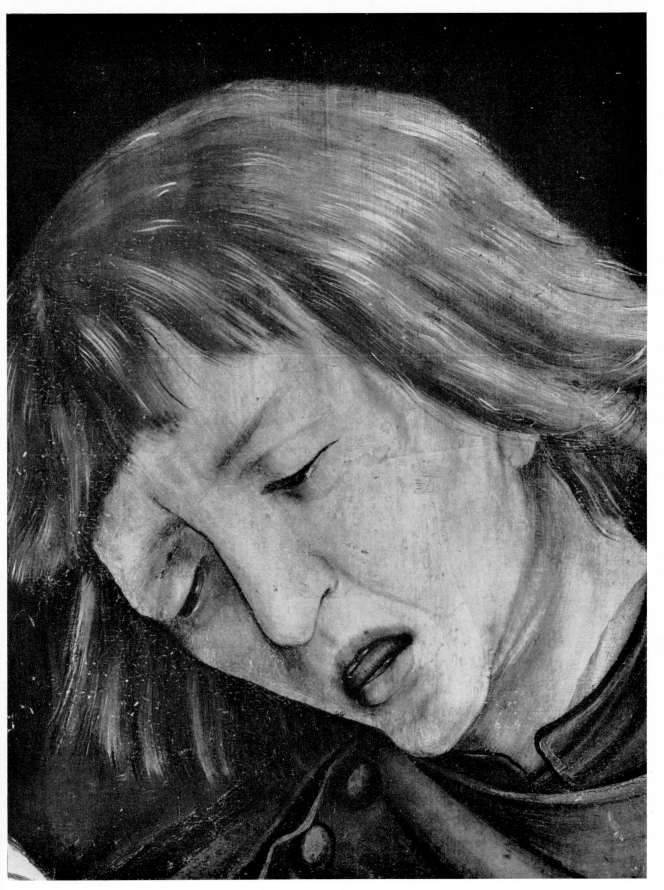

21. *Saint John the Evangelist*. Detail from Plate 16

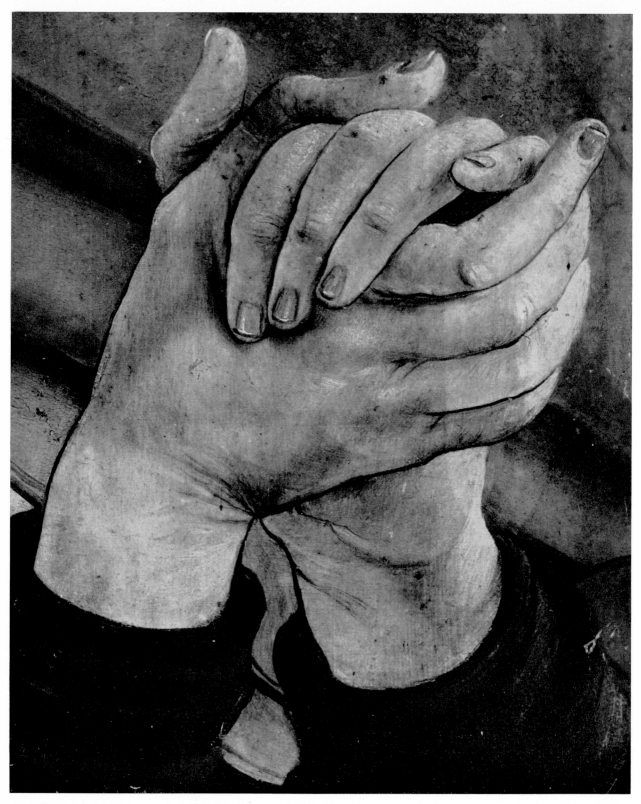

22. *The Hands of the Virgin.* Detail from Plate 16

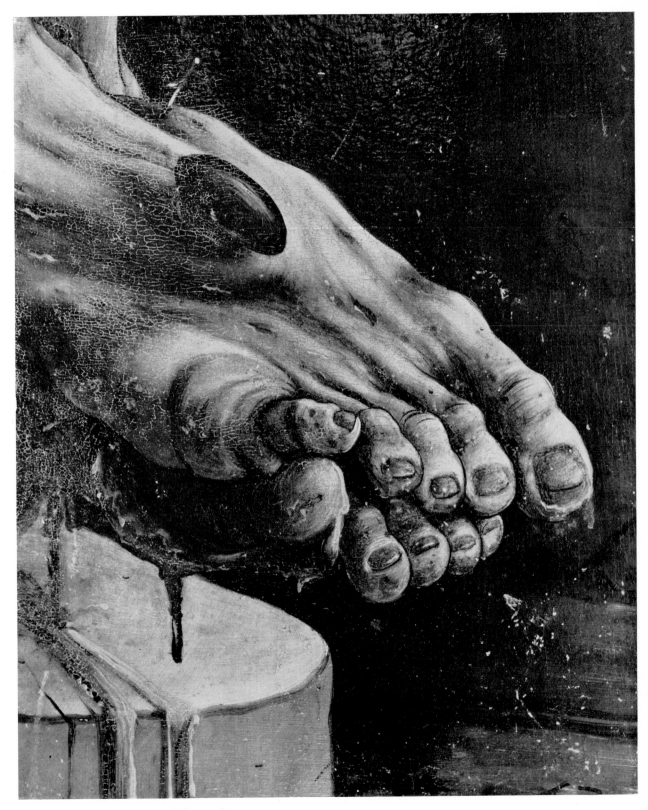

23. *The Feet of Christ*. Detail from Plate 17

24. *Head of Christ*. Detail from Plate 17

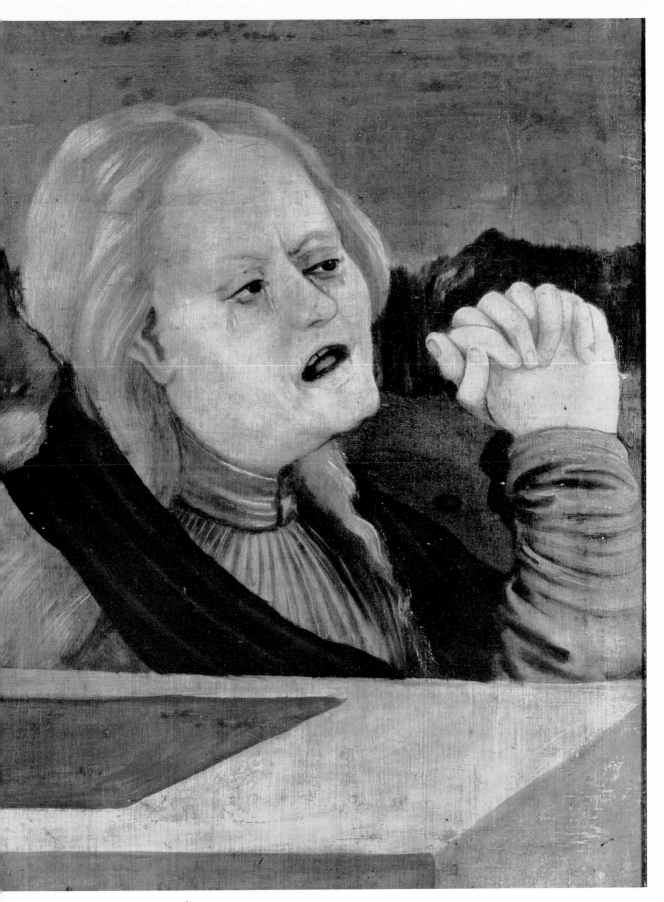

5. *Mary Magdalen*. Detail from Plate 26

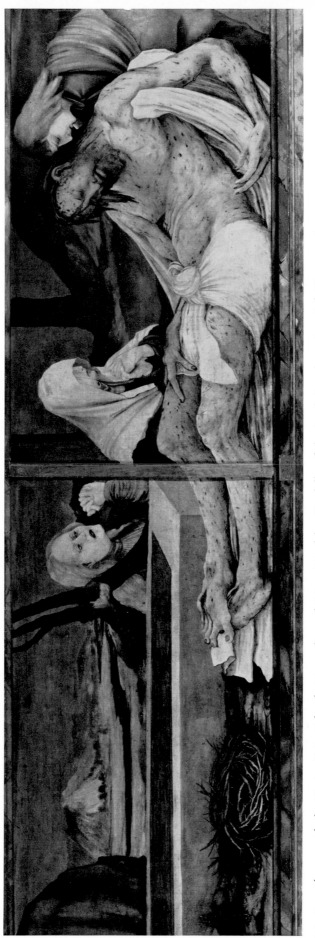

26. *Entombment with the Virgin, Saint John the Evangelist and Mary Magdalen. Predella of the Isenheim altar-piece (cf. Plate 15-D)*

27. *Landscape.* Detail from Plate 26

28. *Saint Anthony*. Left wing of the first stage
of the Isenheim altarpiece (Plate 14–A)

29. *Saint Sebastian*. Right wing of the first stage
of the Isenheim altarpiece (Plate 14–A)

30. *Capital with tendrils*. Detail from Plate 29

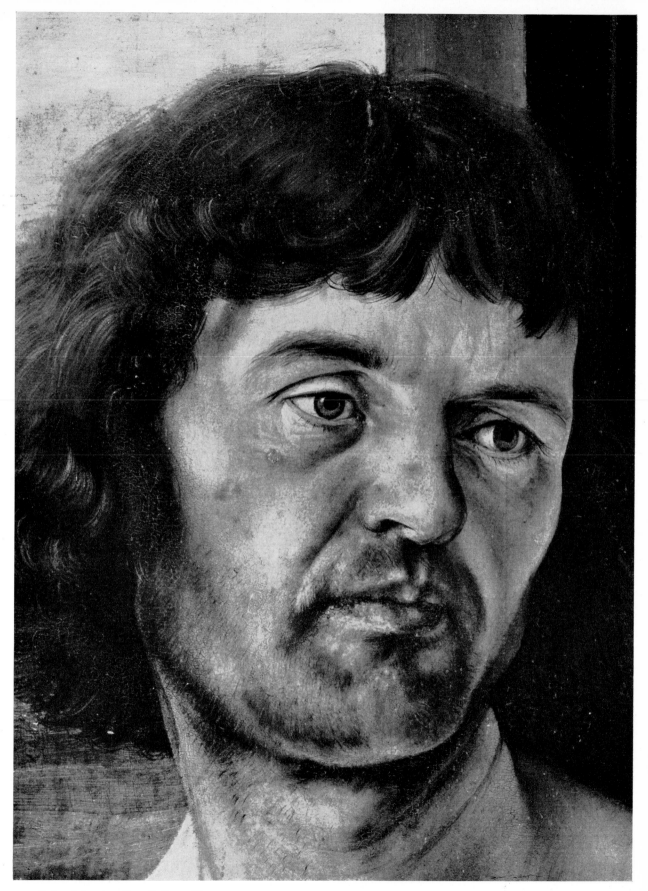

31. *Saint Sebastian*. Detail from Plate 29

32. *The Annunciation.*
Left wing of the second sta[ge]
of the Isenheim altarpiec[e]
(Plate 14–B)

33 (opposit[e])
The Angel of the Annunciati[on]
Detail from Plate

34. *The Prophet Isaiah*. Detail from Plate 32

36–37. *Virgin and Child with Angelic Concert.*

Centre panel of the second stage of the Isenheim altarpiece (Plate 14–B)

38. *Angelic Concert*. Detail from Plate 36

39. *Virgin and Child*. Detail from Plate 37

40. *Statues of Prophets on the Façade of the Chapel.* Detail from Plate 36

41. *The Rose without Thorns*. Detail from Plate 37

42. *Fig Tree*. Detail from Plate 37

43. *Landscape with Monastery and Angels.* Detail from Plate 37

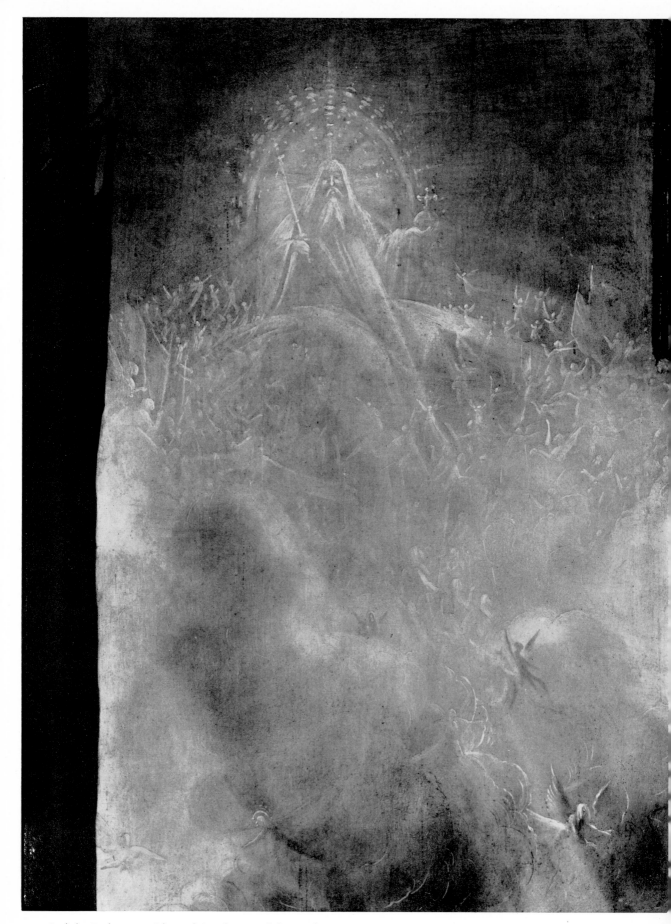

44. *God the Father in a Glory of Angels.* Detail from Plate 37

49. *Saint Paul the Hermit*. Detail from Plate 48

50. *Plants, and the Coat of Arms of the Antonite Preceptor Guido Guersi*. Detail from Plate 48

51. *Plants*. Detail from Plate 48

52. *Saint Anthony with the Stag*. Detail from Plate 48

53. *Deer*. Detail from Plate 48

54. *The Temptation of Saint Anthony*. Right wing of the third stage
    of the Isenheim altarpiece (Plate 15–C)

55. *Devils.* Detail from Plate 54

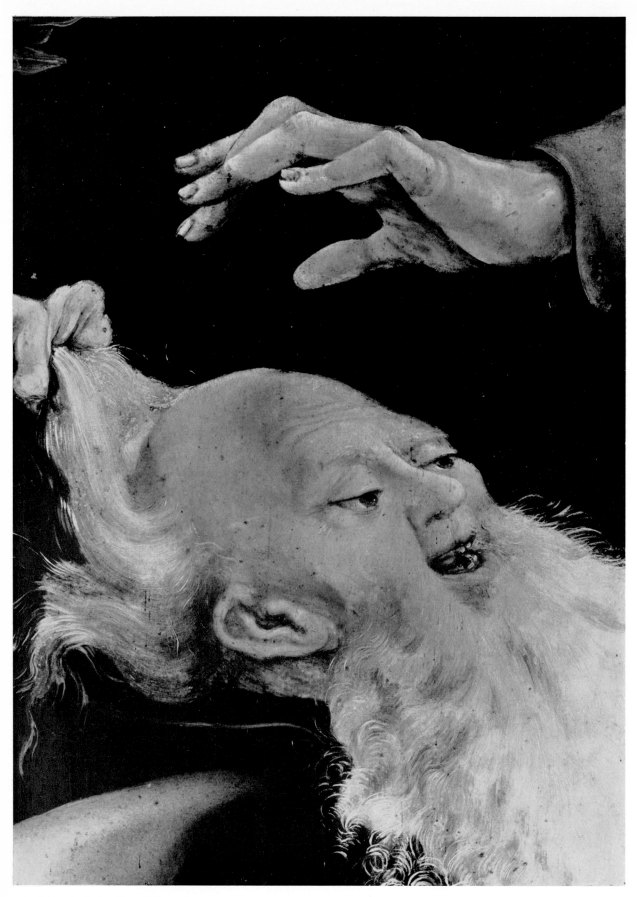

56. *Saint Anthony*. Detail from Plate 54

57. *Bare, mossy Tree*. Detail from Plate 54

58. *Saint Anthony's Fire*. Detail from Plate 54

59. *Demon picking at the Hand of Saint Anthony.* Detail from Plate 54

60. *Christ on the Cross with the Virgin, Saint John and Mary Magdalen.* About 1519. Washington, National Gallery of Art (Samuel H. Kress Collection)

61. *Saint John the Evangelist*. Detail from Plate 60

62. *Madonna in the Garden*. About 1517–19. From the Altarpiece of Our Lady of the Snows. Stuppach near Mergentheim, Parish Church

63. *Landscape and Beehives.* Detail from Plate 62

64. *Still Life*. Detail from Plate 62

65. *Vase with Flowers*. Detail from Plate 62

66. *Church Portal*. Detail from Plate 62

67. *The Miracle of the Snows*. About 1517–19. From the Altarpiece of Our Lady of the Snows. Freiburg im Breisgau, Augustinermuseum

68. *Pope Liberius and the Donors of the Church of S. Maria Maggiore.* Detail from Plate 67

69. *Procession on the Esquiline in Rome.* Detail from Plate 67

70. *Dead Christ*. 1523 (?). Aschaffenburg, Collegiate Church

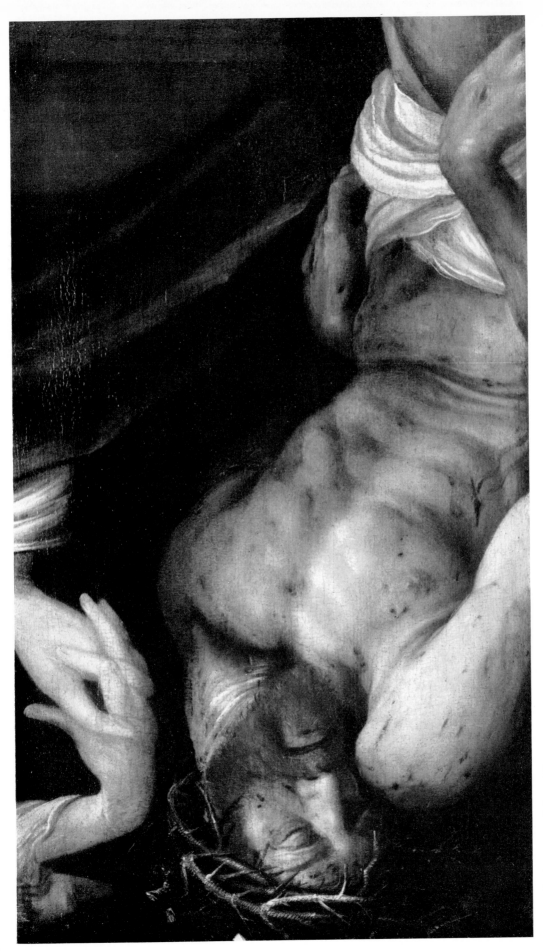

71. *Dead Christ. Detail from Plate 70*

72. *The Disputation of Saints Erasmus and Maurice.* About 1524–1525. Munich, Alte Pinakothek

73. *Saint Maurice*. Detail from Plate 72

74–75. *Gold, Pearls and Embroidery on the Mitre and Chasuble of Saint Erasmus.* Details from Plate 72

ESAIAS
53

...RIST VMB VNSER SVND WILEN GESCLAGEN

76. *The Carrying of the Cross.* About 1526. From the so-called Tauberbischofsheim Altarpiece. Karlsruhe, Kunsthalle

77. *Crucifixion*. About 1526. From the so-called Tauberbischofsheim Altarpiece. Karlsruhe, Kunsthalle

78. *The Virgin*. Detail from Plate 77

79. *Soldiers*. Detail from Plate 76

80. *Christ carrying the Cross*. Detail from Plate 76

NOTES ON THE PLATES

BY EBERHARD RUHMER

THE two introductory essays are taken from books by the French writer Joris-Karl Huysmans (1848–1907), who visited Cassel in 1888 and Colmar in 1903. Both the extract from *Là-bas* and the slightly shortened chapter from *Trois Primitifs* have been newly translated by Dr. Robert Baldick, Oxford. The translation of Dr. Ruhmer's text is by Marguerite Kay.

The paintings in Basel, Colmar, Freiburg and Stuppach have been specially photographed for this publication by Hans Hinz, Basel. The remaining plates have been made from Museum photographs.

We wish to express our gratitude to the following for permission to reproduce paintings in their possession: Öffentliche Kunstsammlung, Basel; Museum Unterlinden, Colmar; Augustinermuseum, Freiburg im Breisgau; Badische Kunsthalle, Karlsruhe; Alte Pinakothek, Munich; National Gallery of Art, Washington; and the Parish authorities of SS. Peter and Alexander, Aschaffenburg, and of the church at Stuppach near Bad Mergentheim.

NOTES ON THE PLATES

I: Plates 1–3

THE MOCKING OF CHRIST

Munich, Pinakothek.

Pinewood, 42⅞ × 29 in. (109 × 73.5 cm.).

Beneath the inscription: ANNO MD III DIE DECEM, removed in 1910, an older one came to light: ANNO M.D. III DI . . XX . . I. DECEMB. This was not autograph either and disappeared during the restoration, but it was in all probability a reliable rendering of the original inscription on a strip at the bottom that had been cut off. This date, 1503, the earliest date on an unquestionably authentic picture by Grünewald, is all the more credible in that in style, technique and colour it is the most archaic of all his surviving paintings.

The 'tabula illussionis Christi' was in a side choir in the collegiate church of Aschaffenburg and was presented to Duke William V of Bavaria, who expressed his thanks for it on 21 June 1613 (Zülch 1938, 96, 323, 380). Subsequently it is alleged to have been in the Carmelite monastery at Munich from whence it passed to the university of that town; 1909 it came to the Pinakothek where it was restored and recognized by Heinz Braune as a work by Grünewald.

In addition to the cut at the bottom mentioned above, the picture suffered further damage in that the eyes in all the heads, with the exception of those of Christ, of the old man, back centre, and of the young man at the back on the extreme right, had been pierced and these had to be restored. Otherwise the picture, particularly as regards the colours, is in good condition.

Copies after the *Mocking of Christ* are in the Aschaffenburg museum and in the Kunstschule of Hanau. The date 1603 (5?) is inscribed on the front of the former copy which bears four coats of arms belonging to the families of v. Cronberg, v. Dehrn, v. Schönborn and v. Landsberg (Zülch 1938, 324). On the back of the wooden panel the occasion for which this copy was made is given as the wedding of Hartmut von Cronberg and Anna Kunigunde von Dehrn, which took place at that time. This is the basis for Zülch's assumption that the donor of the picture, which he regards on the strength of the original inscription

as an epitaph, was the Aschaffenburg vicegerent Johann von Cronberg and that this epitaph was dedicated to his sister Apollonia who died on 23 or 26 Dec. 1503 (Zülch 1938, 324). In 1505 Grünewald delivered a painted epitaph commissioned by Heinrich Reitzmann likewise for the Aschaffenburg collegiate church.

II: Plates 4–11

SS. LAWRENCE, ELIZABETH, CYRIAC AND AN UNKNOWN FEMALE SAINT (LUCY?)

Grisailles on pinewood, 39 × 17 in. (99.1 × 43.2 cm.); 37¾ × 16⅞ in. (95.8 × 42.8 cm.); 38⅞ × 16⅞ in. (98.8 × 43.8 cm.); 39⅞ × 17¼ in. (101.2 × 43.7 cm.).

a and c: Frankfurt a.M., Staedel Kunst-Institut.
b and d: Donaueschingen, Fürstlich Fürstenbergische Gemäldegalerie.

Neither the names of the saints at the bottom of the Frankfurt panels nor the Grünewald signature G in M. N. at the bottom of the *St. Lawrence* are original.

All the pictures come from the Dominican church, Frankfurt, where Sandrart saw them in the XVII century as part of the Heller altarpiece by Dürer: '. . . on the four wings of which on the outside when the altarpiece is closed, this Mattaeus von Aschaffenburg painted these pictures with light in grey and black; on one is St. Lawrence with the grid, on the other a St. Elizabeth, on the third a St. Stephen and on the fourth another picture that has slipped my memory, very prettily set, as can still be seen in Frankfurt' (1675). Then: '. . . on an altar panel the Blessed Elizabeth, St. Stephen, St. Lawrence and R. . . .' (1679). A. A. v. Lersner expresses himself in a similar way (Frankfurt Chronicle I (1706) and II (1734)) and he calls the figure on the fourth picture which had slipped Sandrart's memory, a 'male saint' whereas in the Donaueschingen grisailles, the figure, difficult to identify, is a female saint. The assertion by both that the four saints occupied *four* wings when the altarpiece was closed, is strange. By 1804 SS. *Lawrence* and *Cyriac* were already separated from the female saints; in

1810/12 Sulpiz Boisserée saw and described the former (quoted by Zülch 1938, 392).

It is extremely doubtful whether Sandrart's statement that Mathis painted the grisailles for Dürer's Heller Altarpiece is correct; he merely describes the altarpiece as he saw it in the XVII century: its original appearance, however, is not known.

The uncertainty as to whether Grünewald's grisailles originally formed part of the work by Dürer and his school, is chiefly based on the following observations:

When the altarpiece was closed, Sandrart saw four adjacent wings each with two pictures one above the other. The movable centre pair covered Dürer's main panels: *The Assumption* and *Coronation of the Virgin*. Three panels of these two wings, also cut apart, are in the Historical Museum, Frankfurt. Top right: two figures from an *Adoration of the Magi*, which was continued on the lost upper picture of the left wing. On the lower part of the two movable wings are: right Thomas Aquinas and St. Christopher, left SS. Peter and Paul. These four pictures of the Dürer school are also painted in grisaille (according to Sandrart, 1675: Hans Grünewald = Hans Baldung-Grien). The four grisailles by Grünewald must accordingly have been on the two fixed wings which framed the Dürer school grisailles.

If we reconstruct the (closed) altarpiece in this way optic-aesthetic discordancies are at once obvious. Of Grünewald's saints, the two upper ones stand on socle-like steps, those of Dürer stand considerably lower on the ground. Further if we remember that all the Grünewald grisailles have a piece missing at the top then the two saints – Lawrence and Cyriac – must have stood in addition that much higher than the neighbouring Dürer ones. Moreover Grünewald's St. Cyriac is considerably larger e.g. in the proportions than the immediately adjoining Moor king of Dürer. Most suspicious of all, however, is the fact that each of the four panels by Dürer had two main figures, those of Grünewald only one.

As has already been mentioned the measurements of the two groups of paintings do not correspond at all well. In their present state the Dürer grisailles measure 96×60 cm., whereas the Grünewald grisailles were in any case higher than 101 cm. (*c.* 106?), their width on the other hand is only 43 cm., i.e. higher and much narrower. When the altarpiece was open Grünewald's grisailles must have projected above the polychrome inner sides of the movable wings whilst their width was considerably less.

These discrepancies may have been to some extent adjusted by the cutting down of the panels and a corresponding reframing: it would, however, be paradoxical to assume such difficulties as *a priori* ones. If, as Sandrart maintained, Grünewald had painted his grisailles for the Heller altarpiece together with Dürer (1508/9) or even immediately afterwards, it would have been absurd to coordinate them so badly with the existing ones. It is far more likely that they were originally intended for quite a different purpose and formed the wings of a separate altarpiece that Grünewald is known from documentary evidence to have painted for the same church shortly after the completion of Dürer's Heller altarpiece.

We learn from the documents of the Kemnaten lawsuit 1514/15 that Mathis had painted 'eyn tafel' (a panel) for the Frankfurt Dominican monastery in 1511/12. Sandrart describes this as follows: 'Strange but very praiseworthy is the *Transfiguration of Christ* on Mount Tabor, done in water colours in which in the forefront is an extraordinarily beautiful cloud and in it Moyses and Elijah appear together, with the apostles kneeling on the ground, in invention, colouring and all refinements so very excellently composed that in its uniqueness it is surpassed by nothing, yes it is incomparable in style and character and a mother of all the graces' (1675). And: '. . . the Transfiguration of our Redeemer Jesus Christ on the Mount of Tabor, with Moses and Elijah appearing in the clouds, and there, too, below on the mountain the apostles in a very ecstasy of fear. . . .'

This painting is lost. I think I can demonstrate that the grisaille Saints originally formed part of the *Transfiguration of Christ* and not of the Heller altarpiece but a more detailed discussion of this must wait for another occasion.

Even before 1743 the grisailles must have been cut apart (Salm 1951, 120). After 1800 the Dominican monastery was secularized and the art treasures became the property of the town in 1802, when the Dominican church was for a time adapted as a museum. By 1804 the Donaueschingen panels were no longer in Frankfurt (Salm 1951, 120). In

1808 Carl von Dalberg purchased the Frankfurt paintings and presented them to the Frankfurt Museum Friends and from them the Heller altarpiece passed to the Frankfurt historical museum in 1877. Grünewald's *SS. Lawrence and Cyriac* are now in the Staedel Institute on loan from the historical museum (Prinz, 1957, 8).

The two female saints were recognized in a private collection as works by Grünewald by Julius Wilhelm (Lörrach), Inspector of ancient monuments, and by Irmgard Geissler (Freiburg) and in 1951 were purchased by the Fürstlich Fürstenbergische Gemäldegalerie in Donaueschingen (Christian Altgraf Salm, *Munich Yearbook* 1951, 118 ff.).

The Frankfurt panels are in a considerably better state than the Donaueschingen ones. They are, however, all cut down: *St. Lawrence* at the top, *St. Elizabeth* top and bottom, *St. Cyriac* top and *St. Lucy* (?) top. According to Salm's report the contours of the female saints were gone over in the XIX century, the shadows in the niches were lightened and St. Elizabeth's head scarf overpainted. During the careful restoration of 1952/3 larger areas (such as the cast shadow behind St. Lucy (?)) were entirely repainted. The column sections on the backs are in varying degrees of preservation; only faint traces of the piece at the back of St. Elizabeth can be discerned.

St. Lawrence is represented with his attribute the grid; at the back of his head is a hop branch, below this a spray of mistletoe. St. Elizabeth has a fig branch above her head, on the right at the bottom: bedstraw, agrimony and mallow. Ivy winds round the capital of the column on the backs of the two panels that belong together.

St. Cyriac cures the frenzied princess Artemia, the daughter of Diocletian. On the pages of the open book are the words of the exorcizing formula: AVCT (ORITAT)E D(OMI)NI N(OST)RI IH(S)V X(PHST)I EXORCI(Z)O TE P(ER) ISTA TRIA NO(M)I(N)A EIXAI EN ON(OMA)TI GRAM(M)ATON IN NO(M)I(N)E P(AT)RIS ET FILII ET SP(IRIT)VS S(AN)CTI AMEN. – Fig branches are at the back of St. Cyriac's head. Virginia creeper can be seen above St. Lucy's (?) niche, on the ground mouse-ear chickweed, hieracium, celandine and hawkweed. Virginia creeper winds round the capital of the column at the back of the two panels that belong together

(cf. Christian Altgraf Salm, *Munich Yearbook* 1951, 122).

III: Plates 12–13

CHRIST ON THE CROSS WITH THE THREE MARIES, JOHN THE EVANGELIST AND LONGINUS

Basel, Öffentliche Kunstsammlung.

Limewood, $29\frac{1}{2} \times 21\frac{3}{8}$ in. (75×54.4 cm.).

The words: VERE FILIVS DEI ERAT ISTE (St. Mark, 15, 39) appear between the head and raised arms of Longinus.

The origin cannot be traced back very far. The painting is listed in the inventories of the Basel collection from 1775.

There is a black strip running right round the edge of the panel, the painting is therefore preserved in full. On the other hand bored holes (for hinges) on the right vertical edge suggest that the panel formed the left wing of a triptych (Zülch 1938, 275, 324; Vogt 1957, 157). It is generally assumed that two such panels were on each wing – the surviving one top left. It was undoubtedly an altarpiece of the Passion, the main panel of which must by comparison have measured approximately 160×120 cm. No such panel by Grünewald is, however, known.

The painting is generally regarded as early and dated *c.* 1505; Feurstein alone puts the date forward to '*c.* 1508' (1930, 79); but perhaps even this date is too early. The painting is freer and more sensitive in design, softer in the manner of painting, incomparably more significant in expression even than the grisailles of 1511/12. The chiaroscuro colour is scarcely less masterly than in the Isenheim altarpiece, the *Crucifixion* of which bears the date 1515. The Basel *Christ on the Cross* must probably be placed between the two dates.

On the back, top left, is a pen sketch of foliage ornament; presumably this side too was to have been painted (Zülch 1938, 324).

In the background in the Basel *Crucifixion*: left *The Agony in the Garden*, top left five heads of angels; in the background on the right soldiers moving away (M. Meier 1957, 158) though this is difficult to recognize.

IV: Plates 14–59

THE ISENHEIM ALTARPIECE

Colmar, Museum Unterlinden.

Carved and painted on limewood. Overall measurements originally 26×16½ ft. (8×5 m.).

1st stage: St. Anthony – Crucifixion – St. Sebastian – Predella (Entombment) 91⅜×29½ in. (232×75 cm.); 105⅞×120⅞ in. (269×307 cm.); 91⅜×30⅛ in. (232×76.5 cm.); 26⅜×134¼ in. (67×341 cm.).

2nd stage: Annunciation – Christmas Picture – Resurrection 105⅞×55⅞ in. (269×142 cm.); 104⅜×119⅝ in. (265×304 cm.); 105⅞×56¼ in. (269×143 cm.).

3rd stage: The Hermits – (Carved figures: St. Anthony, St. Augustine, St. Jerome) – Temptation of St. Anthony. Predella (Carved figures, Christ and the twelve Apostles). 104⅜×55½ in. (265×141 cm.); 104⅜×54¾ in. (265×139 cm.).

The date, 1515, is on the Magdalen's ointment box on the *Crucifixion* panel. At the foot of the carved figure of St. Augustine is the portrait of the donor Johann Orliaco, the preceptor of Isenheim, who resigned his post in 1490. Bottom left on the *Two Hermits* panel is the coat of arms of the Antonite preceptor Guido Guersi, who commissioned the paintings. Bottom right on the *Temptation of St. Anthony* panel is the lament (of Anthony and the sick of the Isenheim hospital): *Ubi eras Jhesu bone, ubi eras Quare non affuisti, ut sanares vulnera mea.* On the *Crucifixion* panel, next to John the Baptist is the inscription: ILLVM OPORTET CRESCERE. ME AVTEM MINVI (St. John, 3, 30).
In the church of the Antonite monastery in Isenheim (Alsace) the polyptych stood unsupported on the high altar of the choir which was sealed off from the nave by a reredos. As early as 1656/57 the altarpiece (or a copy of the *Crucifixion*?) seems to have been removed from its original place, at any rate Remigius Fäsch (quoted Zülch 1938, 380 f.) describes a removal to 'Thann . . . for the sake of greater safety'. In 1793/94 the French dismembered the altarpiece in Isenheim, on which occasion the superstructure was destroyed except for a few fragments, which are now in the Colmar museum. Thanks to the Colmar painter L. L. Karpff, called Kasimir, the paintings and sculpture were saved from similar destruction. To begin with they were lodged in the Colmar Jesuit college, then, in 1852, in the chapel of the Unterlinden monastery.
According to H. A. Schmid (1911, 133 f.) their condition is generally very good, but the background in the Crucifixion panel was largely destroyed and restored 'without real understanding'. As against this, however, it should be noted that the landscape shows the greatest similarity to that of the Basel *Crucifixion*. For the rest the Isenheim altarpiece contains an unusual number of pentimenti which give interesting insight into Grünewald's method of working. Thus the Head of Christ was not originally brought down so low, whilst the right upper arm – which was altered at least three times – was drawn up. The Virgin originally stood up straight, the drapery fell diagonally to the back, her eyes were open and fixed on Christ. St. John was not holding her, his right arm and hand have been altered several times. The same applies to the head of Mary Magdalen. St. John the Baptist's outstretched index finger was not originally bent up so much.
In the XVI and XVII centuries the Isenheim altarpiece was known as a work by Grünewald. Thus Bernhard Jobin describes it in 1573 as 'köstlich gemäl zu Issna' (beautifully painted at Issna) by 'Mathis von Oschnaburg' (i.e. Aschaffenburg), and similarly in 1657/67 Remigius Fäsch (Zülch 1938, 380 f.). Sandrart only mentions the single figure of St. Anthony from the Isenheim altarpiece – he calls the place where it stood 'Eysenach' –(1675, 1683), but he knows the whole as a work by Grünewald. On the other hand the altarpiece is mentioned in French sources as a work by Dürer (cf. Zülch 1938, 381) and as such it was regarded during the whole of the XVIII century (cf. Zülch 1938, 385). At the beginning of the XIX century Sulpiz Boisserée began to doubt Dürer's authorship; he noted the connection between the Isenheim altarpiece and the Frankfurt panels. In 1820 C. M. Engelhardt considered the Isenheim altarpiece to be a collective work by Dürer and Grünewald, attributing to the latter the *Crucifixion*, the *Annunciation*, the *Resurrection* and the *Entombment* (H. A. Schmid 1911, 364, 366). Jacob Burckhardt was the first to reclaim the entire altarpiece for Grünewald (Stuttgart Kunstblatt, 1844, 151; quoted H. A. Schmid 1911, 369).

With regard to the carvings, the predella is by Desiderius Beychel whereas the three statues – SS. Anthony, Augustine with the donor, and Jerome – are ascribed to the Strassburg sculptor Niclas Hagnower (W. Voge, *Niclas Hagnower*, Freiburg 1930). Two *Peasants offering Sacrifices*, who originally probably knelt at the feet of St. Anthony, later passed to the Böhler collection, Munich.

The preceptor Johann von Orliaco donated the carved altarpiece; this work must have been completed by 1505. Orliaco's successor in office, Guido Guersi, commissioned the paintings. The *Crucifixion* seems to be dated '1515' (date on the Magdalen's ointment box). But Grünewald's work must have taken a considerable time. In 1513 and 1515 he signed contracts, the contents of which are not known, with an Alsatian carpenter or carver Michael Wesser; it is not impossible that these had some connection with the Isenheim altarpiece. Grünewald's documented absences from Mainfranken in 1514/15 and in 1516 suggest to Zülch that during those periods Mathis was in Isenheim. Since the preceptor Guersi died in February 1516 and Grünewald again entered the service of the court, work on the Isenheim altarpiece must of necessity have been finished in 1516. It is not possible to say how much before 1515, the date on the *Crucifixion*, work began. It is very unlikely that Grünewald painted the panels at Isenheim because during the period 1513/16 he also had commissions in Mainfranken.

The Isenheim *Crucifixion* is closely akin to the small one in Basel. The *Temptation of St. Anthony*, however, which was particularly emphasized by older writers, is right outside Grünewald's own field: this composition has a definite predecessor in the small picture in the Galleria Doria, Rome, by the Paduan painter Parentino (*c.* 1437/1531), but Grünewald's composition has the sides reversed which suggests an engraving as mediator between the Italian painting and the German one. A few German prints which precede Grünewald's panel are more loosely connected with the composition: the engraving by Schongauer on which the saint is being lifted into the skies by the demons, and the woodcut *The Seven Deadly Sins* by Hans Baldung-Grien, 1511. Later this same Baldung designed a similar *Temptation of St. Anthony* for a glass window in the Freiburg minster (Locherer chapel), which was executed *c.* 1520 in the Ropstein workshop (now on loan in the Augustinermuseum).

It may be mentioned here that the paintings of the Isenheim altarpiece were more rarely copied than some of Grünewald's other works. An old copy was owned about the middle of the XVII century by Herr von der Gruss in Bottmingen (Zülch 1938, 381).

One of the main concerns of Grünewald research is to uncover literary sources which might have guided or influenced the artist for the Isenheim altarpiece and for other unusual compositions. Here, too, it was the donor's privilege and duty to determine the subjects down to the last detail. With regard to the Isenheim altarpiece a certain amount can be explained by the locality for which it was made, by the special significance of this altar and by the very natural and personal wishes of the donors Johann von Orliaco and Guido Guersi, preceptors of the Antonite monastery in Isenheim, in the hospital of which patients were treated for epilepsy, blood and skin diseases. The high altar of the church was the first stage of the healing programme: the patient was taken to it to begin with, to assure him the possibility of participating in a miracle. Only after this did the medical treatment begin. The chief saints of the order were St. Anthony (invoked against St. Anthony's fever, Ergot poisoning), St. Sebastian (against the plague), SS. John the Evangelist and the Baptist (against epilepsy). St. Anthony as titular saint is enthroned in the carved central shrine on the third stage. SS. Anthony and Sebastian as large single figures adorn the wings on the first stage; the two St. Johns are united on the *Crucifixion* panel. The whole altarpiece, however, according to Zülch (1938, 142), was dedicated to the Virgin who dominates the second stage.

It is no mere chance that the Isenheim monastery was in a position to commission one of the largest and most elaborate altarpieces of the day. Although a mendicant order, the Antonites controlled vast funds. According to Zülch (1938, 132) all preceptors of the German Antonite monasteries were of aristocratic descent, highly educated (especially in medicine); only Frenchmen or Italians administered this high office. Since 1477 the Isenheim monastery had been one of the central Houses and Orliaco held the rank of general preceptor for Germany.

Although the *Annunciation* adheres fully to convention, the *Temptation of St. Anthony*, as we have seen, forms part of a pictorial tradition, and the *Resurrection* owes its exceptional impact to Grünewald's own artistic invention and achievement: the etherializing of Christ's Body in colour and light, whilst the *Two Hermits* (visit of St. Anthony aged 90 to St. Paul aged 113) illustrates a story of the Golden Legend, we are unable to trace an immediate source for the idea and composition of the two main panels, the *Christmas Picture* and the *Crucifixion*.

Heinrich Feurstein (Bonn 1930) was the first to point out that certain moods and pictorial elements in these two compositions reflect something of a literary work of mystic content: the Revelations of St. Bridget of Sweden (1303/73). This was first published in 1492 in Lübeck; in 1502 a German edition was published by Koberger in Nürnberg entitled *Das Puch der himmlischen Offenbarung der hl. Wittiben Birgitta von dem Kunigreich Sweden*. Awful threats of perdition appear in the visions of the saint; in view of the activities of the popes at Avignon, fiercely attacked also by Petrarch, of the corrupted conditions everywhere in the church, she prophesies the downfall of the church and yearns for a reformation. Alongside the sombre burning mood of these visions are crassly realistic pictures (Vogt 1957, 21 f.) expressed in a stark cruel language.

Certain striking details in the *Crucifixion* – a kind of religious allegory – can be directly matched with words of St. Bridget: 'Thou art the Lamb that John pointed out with his finger,' or 'His feet were curled round the nails as round door hinges towards the other side,' and so on.

Even more frequent and closer are the links between text and painting in the *Christmas Picture*. A whole bibliography exists on the picture of the Incarnation which has assumed overwhelming proportions and which, by the very nature of the material, can be spun out indefinitely. M. Meier has given a masterly survey of all the credible interpretations in his Grünewald book (1957, 160 f.) and because of its reliable objectivity we quote it here verbatim:

'It is quite evident that here, too, as in the *Crucifixion*, it is not the historical event that is depicted but the symbolic significance of the Incarnation of Christ and the glorification of the Mother of God. Feurstein gives a summary of the attempted interpretations – in the meantime new ones have been added – and he was also the first to point to the Revelations of St. Bridget of Sweden in the "Sermo angelicus" as the source not only of this picture but of the whole altarpiece. At that time these revelations had a popular significance so that their use as a basis for the content of the Isenheim work is more plausible than all the learned liturgical interpretations of J. Bernhart (*Die Symbolik im Menschwerdungsbild des Isenheimer Altars*, Munich, 1921). According to Feurstein the Virgin Annunciate is represented on the left at the end of the Old Covenant in the "house and temple of Solomon before the new age of fulfilment", on the right the symbol of the New Covenant, the fulfilment of the promise that God is to be born into the world as a human being. Thus the figure in the temple inclined towards the centre adorned with a celestial crown must be understood as "Maria aeterna, decreed by God before the Creation to be the Mother of God, in a state of expectation and as leader of the waiting ones, created from the sum total of the Legends of the Virgin". The glass jug on the step is the symbol of virginity, the objects of the lying-in-room are symbols of the humiliation on earth of the Son of God. Mary sits in the Hortus Conclusus, the walled garden. She is the "rose without thorns" (represented next to her on the right), the "house of God" (the church in the background). It is not possible to explain the whole of the Christmas panel by the Revelations of St. Bridget. Many other sources, unknown to us, were certainly alive in Mathis's imagination and through the intensity of his artistic vision were assimilated to an indissoluble whole.'

V: Plates 60–61

CHRIST ON THE CROSS WITH ST. JOHN THE EVANGELIST, THE VIRGIN, AND MARY MAGDALEN

Washington, National Gallery of Art, Samuel H. Kress Collection.

Limewood, 24¼×18⅛ in. (61.5×46 cm.).

Signed: m.g. (top right, next to the ring from which the inscription plaque is suspended).

In 1526 the panel – a painted epitaph – may have belonged to canon Caspar Schantz of Aschaffenburg and from him it passed first to Heinrich Reitzmann, then to Georg Schantz. Sandrart saw the panel about 1640/50 in the collection of the Elector Maximilian of Bavaria. It was allegedly destroyed in the fire at the Munich residence but reappeared in 1922 in the collection of councillor Schoene in Essen. Between 1922/38 it was in the F. Koenigs collection, Haarlem, and from 1940 has been in the Samuel H. Kress collection.

Pentimenti have been noted on the hands of the Virgin and St. John and on the head and feet of the Baptist, on Christ's loin cloth and on Mary's drapery. The figure of the Magdalen seen from the back was apparently originally the furthest forward, cutting off a small part of the figure of the Virgin; not till later did Grünewald move the figure of the Virgin in front of Mary Magdalen.

It can be deduced from the many copies that the little panel has been cut by just over 1 cm. all round. When the painting reappeared in 1922 it was described as badly damaged and by 1936 had been twice restored. In 1938 the Cologne restorer Otto Klein removed several layers of overpainting (only the body of Christ and the faces had been left untouched) and cleaned it thoroughly, whereby the very detailed landscape, light beneath a dark sky, known from the copies, re-emerged from the formerly almost black background. At the same time certain restorations were undertaken (Zülch 1938, 123, 325 f.).

Sandrart had already re-discovered the panel as a work by Grünewald; he writes: 'Further his royal highness Duke Wilhelm in Bavaria of blessed memory, an understanding judge and art lover, had a small *Crucifixion* with Our Lady and St. John as well as a kneeling and reverently praying Mary Magdalen, painted with the utmost care by this hand and he loved it dearly without knowing by whom it was; the same, owing to the marvellous Christ on the Cross hanging so convincingly and resting on the feet, is very unusual, so that life itself could not produce a better and if we muse over it long and patiently enough we find it natural above all other *Crucifixions*. For that reason, by gracious command of the noble duke, Raphael Sadeler engraved it on copper in the year 1605 the size of a half sheet, and afterwards his royal highness Maximilian of blessed

memory was mightily pleased when I revealed the master's name to him' (1675).

The date is highly controversial and varies between 'very early' and 'very late'. Quite certainly both extremes are wrong. It is equally far removed from the early style as represented in the Munich *Mocking of Christ* of 1503 and from the late style as it appears in the Karlsruhe Passion panel of 1526/27. Rather in the developed maturity of mood and in the freedom and breadth of the painting is it close to the Isenheim altarpiece (*c.* 1515). Stylistically, however, it is even closer to the *Miracle of the Snows* in Freiburg of 1519. We need only note the strange, uncertain attitudes and gestures, the elongated bodies and heads, the mannerist detachment of the miming expressions, the dense almost straight *ductus*, apparent in the folds of the drapery, which in the earliest and latest styles is more ample and more powerful. The strong chiaroscuro which produces greater colour harmonies than in the *Miracle of the Snows* is self-explanatory in view of the subject matter. We should therefore suggest the date: about 1519 (Feurstein also gives the date '*c.* 1519/20', 1930, 72 ff., 117 ff.).

Raphael Sadeler's engraving of 1605 is the earliest copy of this, Grünewald's most famous painting in the XVII century. At least sixteen copies in a wide variety of techniques were made during the Baroque period, nearly all probably based on the engraving.

VI: Plates 62–69

MARIA-SCHNEE (OUR LADY OF THE SNOWS) ALTARPIECE:

(A) MADONNA IN THE GARDEN

Stuppach near Mergentheim (Württemberg), Parish Church.

Pinewood, lined with canvas, $72\frac{7}{8} \times 59$ in. (185×150 cm.).

(B) THE MIRACLE OF THE SNOWS

Freiburg i. Br., Augustiner Museum.

Pinewood, $70\frac{1}{2} \times 36$ in. (179×91.5 cm.).

The frame of the 'Maria Schnee' altarpiece, undoubtedly designed by Grünewald and executed in his workshop, from which sculptured works were repeatedly commissioned, still remains in its original place in the Three Magi or Maria Schnee chapel of the Aschaffenburg collegiate church. On the base is the inscription: AD HONOREM . FESTI . NIVIS . DEIPAERAE . VIRGINIS . HENRICHVS . RETZMAN . HVIVS . AEDIS . CVSTOS . ET/CANONICVS . AC . GASPAR SCHANTZ CANONICVS . EIVSDEM. E. C. 1519. On the right Grünewald's monogram G in M with N above. On the lunette arch: . MARIA . MATER . GRACIE . MATER . MISERICORDIE . TV . NOS . AB . HOSTE . PROT. – In the lunette: AD DIVAM/MARIAM VIRGINEM DE NIVE/ASPICE MORTALES PLACIDIS PIA/MATER, OCVLIS/EXCRVCIANT VARIIS QVOS SVA FATA MODIS.

According to his testament of 5 August 1514 canon Heinrich Reitzmann had already in 1513 commissioned from Grünewald in Seligenstadt an altarpiece with the miracle of the snows at S. Maria Maggiore for the chapel of the brothers Caspar and Georg Schantz in the collegiate church of Aschaffenburg: '. . . festum Nivis gloriosissime Marie virginis' (Zülch 1938, 358). According to the consecration panel with the coat of arms of cardinal Albrecht, preserved in the chapel, the consecration of chapel and altar took place in November 1516. In 1517 the tabula, so we hear, is ready and the colours prepared. Perhaps Grünewald began at that time the work which, according to the date on the surviving frame, was completed by 1519. Judging by the measurements and proportions of the frame and by the wing panel painted on both sides we should expect a triptych with movable wings and the fixed central panel twice as large as the surviving right one (the scene on the back of which obviously required a continuation to the left) i.e. c. 180×190 cm. There is one panel by Grünewald that corresponds at least to the conjectured height and cannot be linked with any other known work, namely the Stuppach Madonna which, accordingly, has often been claimed as the central panel of the Aschaffenburg Miracle of the Snows altarpiece, even though it is considerably narrower (only 150 cm.) and unlike the Freiburg panel is lined with canvas. In actual fact there are even more reasons for accepting the Stuppach Madonna, the origin of which is lost in obscurity, than have previously been put forward. The reverse of the Miracle of the Snows in Freiburg shows the right half of an Adoration of the Magi, i.e.

the figures of the three Magi. This Adoration, of which the left half is lost, has been wrongly regarded as a work of inferior quality by a master of about 1530. In my opinion the relation to Grünewald is very close, but the discussion of the entire problem and the reconstruction of the altarpiece must be left for a special article.

The altarpiece seems to have been dismembered as early as the XVI century, according to Zülch (1938, 233) in Grünewald's lifetime and in connection with the peasant rising of 1525.

Until the beginning of the XIX century the Miracle of the Snows was in the Aschaffenburg collegiate church. In 1828 it passed to the Munich gallery where it was sold by auction in 1852. After several changes of ownership it finally in 1904 came to Freiburg as a donation. The state of the painting, restored by P. Huber in 1924 (Zülch 1938, 328), is not perfect, particularly as regards the colours. Next to the dominant red tones the blues and greens stand out individually and unrelated. The technique is given as tempera and resin. Grünewald probably achieved the warmth and intensity that is now lacking by using coloured glazings which have been lost. Various damages can be seen.

The origin of the Stuppach Madonna cannot be traced back very far. The cult of the Velamen, the 'miraculous veil' that the Virgin Mary holds, was established, according to Schmid and Zülch (1938, 245), in Tauberbischofsheim, Aachen and Cologne but not in Aschaffenburg so that Tauberbischofsheim (the place of origin of Grünewald's Karlsruhe Passion panels, the measurements of which are certainly similar) has been considered as the original home of the Stuppach Madonna. Be that as it may, by 1809 it was in Mergentheim when it was purchased by vicar Blumhofer of Stuppach who placed it on the high altar of his church (Zülch 1938, 328).

When at the beginning of the XX century attention was drawn to the picture it was in the most appalling state and had been distorted by romantic overpainting. In 1926/30 it was restored in the Stuttgart gallery by a painter Tettenborn under the supervision of a commission of experts (cf. also Klaus Graf v. Baudissin, Die Wiederherstellung der Stuppacher Madonna, Kunstchronik 44 (1930), 37; Ulrich Nicolai, Die Restauration der Stuppacher Maria, Kunst und Antiquitätenrundschau 28 (1930), 11).

During the XIX century, the Stuppach Madonna was regarded as a work by Rubens; not until 1907 did Konrad Lange recognize the hand of Grünewald (Meier 1957, 162).

The Freiburg *Miracle of the Snows* seemed to Sulpiz Boisserée about 1810 to be 'remotely connected with Baldung-Grien' (Zülch 1938, 391); in 1897 the art historian Bayersdorfer discovered the authorship of Grünewald.

Attempts have been made by Grünewald scholars to find a more profound interpretation for the Stuppach Madonna, though on the face of it and within the framework of the Virgin in the Meadow type it seems in no way unusual. Here, too, the Revelations of St. Bridget (Book IV, chap. 78) are regarded as the inspiring literary source. According to Feurstein the 'Mother of God is represented as guardian of the church in gravest danger'. The rainbow above the Virgin's head and the church in the background on the right (associated with the south front of Strassburg minster: Naumann 1930, 86, n. 8) are the symbols used by St. Bridget, the beehive and the closed garden gate in the background, left, are common symbols of the Virgin, the low figtree on the left recalls Christ's parable of the figtree. The Virgin Mary, the church of the Virgin Mary and the beehive represent the 'triple House of God'. According to Zülch (1938, 21) the landscape shows the view of the town, waterway with dam and mill and distant mountains, that Grünewald had from the Seligenstadt brook he had leased in 1509 and still owned in 1520.

The following details refer to the subject matter of the *Miracle of the Snows* panel: in 1512 Uriel von Gemmingen introduced the 'Maria-Schnee' cult in the archbishopric of Mainz. On 12 May 1515, Heinrich Reitzmann the donor had his petition for the festival of Our Lady of the Snows 'Historia de festo nivis' printed in Basel by Jacob von Pfortzheim (Zülch 1938, 328). He had been in Rome and had taken part in the festival in S. Maria Maggiore (Zülch 233). According to the legend, the Roman citizen John, who was considering the donation of a church to the Virgin, dreamed on the night of 3/4 August in the year 352 that Our Lady had caused snow to fall on a certain spot on the Esquilin in order to reveal the building site for the promised church. Pope Liberius (represented in the background left, sleeping in an open room) had the same dream the same night.

He immediately ordered a procession to go to the spot seen in the dream and there they found the fallen snow. Using a tool he had brought with him the Holy Father dug up the first spade-full with his own hand: this is the chief scene on the Freiburg panel. On the left the patrician John (with the features of the St. Paul of the *Two Hermits* on the Isenheim altarpiece and related to the Erlangen 'self-portrait' drawing) kneels with his wife.

According to H. A. Schmid the view here is taken from S. Maria Maggiore onto the Lateran palace and Lateran basilica (obviously based on old Roman views); on the left is a city gate in the old Roman wall.

VII: Plates 70–71

DEAD CHRIST

Aschaffenburg, Collegiate Church.

Pinewood, $14\frac{1}{8} \times 53\frac{1}{2}$ in. (36 × 136 cm.).

Left the arms of Cardinal Albrecht, right the arms of one of his predecessors: count Dietrich von Erlach, archbishop of Mainz until 1459.

Whether or not the panel was always in the collegiate church of Aschaffenburg is doubtful. In any case Sulpiz Boisserée, at all times the most careful of observers, does not appear to have seen it there when he visited the church in 1810 and described its art treasures (cf. Zülch 1938, 270).

Count Dietrich von Erlach is buried in the collegiate church at Aschaffenburg; but he was also the first donor of the Holy Sepulchre Chapel of the Grey Sisters in the Aschaffenburg 'Tiergarten', which was completed by Cardinal Albrecht before 1528 (?) (Zülch 1938, 331).

The common interest of the two men whose arms are on the panel might lead one to suppose that the *Dead Christ* was originally painted for the Holy Sepulchre Chapel in the Tiergarten. The Grey Sisters, however, also used another 'Holy Sepulchre' chapel, the donor of which was Dietrich von Erbach, and this one was in the church of S. Agatha, Aschaffenburg (Zülch 1938, 270).

As a matter of fact a number of art treasures in the Aschaffenburg collegiate church come from the collegiate church of Halle and Cardinal Albrecht had the majority of the altarpieces removed from the latter and transferred to the former church when he left Halle in 1539/40.

The arms of Dietrich, who was not – like Albrecht – also archbishop of Magdeburg (Residence at Halle) seem to preclude such a provenance. But it has often been noted that the coat of arms has been overpainted. The restorer Mr. Lohe, Munich, drew my attention to the fact that originally there was only *one* star in the upper right-hand corner and on the left a star instead of the wheel.

An X-ray photograph, recently taken in Munich where the picture is being restored, gives us more detailed insight into the origin of the work. Obviously the composition was once different. Christ was stretched out flat on the ground as in the painting by Hans Holbein the younger in Basel; He was thus originally fully, and not as now only partially, visible. His head was facing almost to the front, His right leg was half covered. To the small head between the Head of Christ and the hands of the Virgin belonged another hand that rested on Christ's left shoulder, approximately on the spot where the hands – not there originally – of the large mourning Virgin now are. Just as the coat of arms already mentioned was originally different so was the cap of the guard belonging to it. The guard on the left did not originally squint upwards but stared straight ahead. It seems that neither the cardinal's hat on the cross above the left coat of arms nor the stem of the Cross with the ladder were present in the first version. Finally, the X-ray reveals a wide valley landscape with towering rocks and low-hanging portions of the sky.

A careful examination enables us to distinguish, broadly speaking, three different stages in the painting (if not more: Christ's right leg e.g. has been altered more than once). It is quite certain that the figure of Christ as it was originally was not by Grünewald but of an earlier date. Christ in His present form, the existing part of the Virgin, the small mourning Magdalen on the right and the arms of Cardinal Albrecht are all without a shadow of doubt by Grünewald himself. The rest is close to him: the fragment of the Cross and ladder, the two guards on the left and right and the overpainted arms on the right; but the painting in these parts is not over-subtle, there is something disagreeable in the expression of the guard on the left. Perhaps Grünewald him-

self only executed the most important and difficult parts of the cardinal's commission, which on formal grounds was not particularly interesting.

A copy, now lost, of a similar painting by Grünewald bore the date 1523 (Zülch 1938, 344); in the same year the decoration of the collegiate church of Halle was begun. As early as 1525 the *Dead Christ* is recorded there.

VIII: Plates 72–75

THE DISPUTATION OF SS. ERASMUS AND MAURICE

Munich, Pinakothek.

Pinewood, 89×69¼ in. (226×176 cm.).

St. Erasmus is a portrait of the donor Cardinal Albrecht. At the bottom of the alb the arms of the archbishoprics of Mainz and Magdeburg and of the bishopric of Halberstadt are embroidered in pearls. According to Grote (*Erasmus-Mauritius-Tafel*, Stuttgart 1957, 4), the head of the prelate between the two saints represents John Ryder, the first provost of the new abbey in Halle, founded in 1519.

The painting comes from the Halle collegiate church which was consecrated in 1523 though the painted and sculptured decoration was not ready until 1526. Grünewald's panel is mentioned in the church inventory of 3 October 1525: 'Uff dem altar Mauricij, an des prosts seitten, im auffgange: Eyne kunstliche gemahlte taffel mit sanct Moritz und sanct Erasmo, etc.' (an artistically painted panel with SS. Maurice and Erasmus on the provost's side on the altar dedicated to St. Maurice). A more accurate idea of the position of the altar can be gained from a document of 1540 (P. Redlich, *Card. Albrecht*, Mainz 1900, 172, 346, supplement 40 a): '. . . die zwei grosse Taffelln uff beyde altaria in den abseyten, als sancti Mauritii und der ander Marie Magdalene. . . .' (The two large panels on the altars in the side apses, one St. Maurice, the other Mary Magdalen.) It is not clear which the provost's side was, but presumably it was the side adjoining the new abbey. In that case the *Disputation* panel was on the altar of the south aisle and the companion piece on the one in the North aisle.

Both panels belonged to altarpieces with wings. Documentary evidence suggests that they formed the culminating points of two cycles of Passion panels which covered the end walls on the north and south sides, 13 panels on each wall. Associated with these 28 panels was a 29th – probably on the West wall – a representation of the *Last Judgement*. All these pictures, a number of which can still be traced (particularly in Aschaffenburg), came from the Cranach workshop. The wings of Grünewald's *Disputation* panel also originated there; they are preserved in the Aschaffenburg Staatsgemäldegalerie. On four panels (deriving from two severed wings) each measuring 233 ×76 cm. are single figures of SS. Lazarus, Mary Magdalen, Martha and Chrysostom, the work of Simon Franck (so-called psuedo-Grünewald), Grünewald's successor in the service of the court (Max J. Friedländer, *Cranach*, Berlin 1932, Pl. 360). If Grünewald left court-service in 1526 and Franck is not established as working for Albrecht in Halle before 1529, then Grünewald's altarpiece must in any case have been enlarged and completed after 1526.

In addition to Grünewald's panel two metal candlesticks, and a candle lighter with the picture of an angel stood on the St. Maurice altar. Three lamps were suspended in front of it (Grote, *Erasmus-Mauritius-Tafel*, Stuttgart 1957, 13).

In 1540 Cardinal Albrecht had the two altarpieces with wings transferred to his 'house' and from there to Aschaffenburg. After 1610 the *Disputation* panel was in the new palace there. It came to Munich about 1820/30 and has been in the Pinakothek since 1836.

Comparatively speaking the condition of the *Disputation* panel is very good. Here too Grünewald did not immediately achieve the final version. Mr. Lohe, the restorer, pointed out to me that the provost for example originally wore a red cap. No cutting down was observed, but it has not been possible to recheck this. The composition is slightly lopsided, unusual in Grünewald's late work. The whole emphasis is on the left side where the figure of St. Erasmus seems pushed close to the edge, while the scene recedes into the distance on the right and is swallowed up in shadow. Seeing that in this, his latest period, Grünewald favoured exactly balanced compositions (cf. the two passion panels in Karlsruhe) we should expect a continuation to the left and at least one figure to counterbalance the archer on the right.

From Sulpiz Boisserée's description (Zülch 1938, 392) we can assume that the picture 'passed as Grünewald' at the beginning of the XIX century, whereas in Boisserée's opinion 'it obviously has all the characteristics of a Hans Baldung-Grien'. But the old attribution to Grünewald has been rightly retained.

The saint standing on the left is identified by the windlass and intestines in his right hand as Erasmus. His features are those of Cardinal Albrecht, allegedly borrowed by Grünewald from Dürer's engraving the *Little Cardinal* of 1519. It should be noted that this very engraving together with autograph drawings by Grünewald were owned by his friend the silk embroiderer Hans Plock, who had probably received them from the artist and kept them in his Luther bible of 1541 (cf. W. Stengel, *Zeitschrift für Kunstwissenschaft* 1952, 65).

Albrecht had had the bones of St. Erasmus brought from Magdeburg to Halle in 1516. He acquired the saint's head from the monastery Olivia near Danzig. Subsequently the cardinal collected additional relics so that the Halle 'Heiltum' (sanctuary) was finally able to muster some 6000 relics – it was called the 'idol of Halle' by Luther and was a main focus for attack during the Reformation. Erasmus became the patron of the new abbey which was intended to devote itself to scholarly study and, as bastion of the old catholic church, to oppose Lutheran Wittenberg. The selection of this patron, the namesake of Erasmus of Rotterdam, for the abbey was a tribute by Albrecht to the great humanist whom he admired and hoped to win over for his new foundation.

On the mitre, exquisitely embroidered in pearls – the work, according to his own testimony, of Hans Plock – are St. Maurice, the oldest patron of the archbishopric, patron of the new abbey and of the town of Halle, and St. Nicolas of Myra (W. Stengel, *Zeitschrift für Kunstwissenschaft* 1952, 73). On the amice, also embroidered in gold and pearls, is Mary Magdalen, the patroness of the archbishopric, in half-length with her ointment box. On the alb (it, too the work of Hans Plock, Stengel 1952, 77) are the arms of the archbishoprics of Mainz and Magdeburg and of the bishopric of Halberstadt embroidered in a similar manner. Except for the late-Gothic staff and tabernacle containing a full-length figure of the Virgin ascribed to the early XV century, all these decorative details are uniform in style, a style that reappears in many of the reliquary shrines, limbs, busts, statues and statuettes of the 'Heiltum' all of which date from the time (1516/26) when Grünewald was supervisor of the cardinal's artistic projects, including those connected with the minor arts and architecture.

St. Maurice, patron saint of the archbishopric of Magdeburg, was chosen by Albrecht as second patron of his new abbey. The painting shows a meeting between the two men which is not historical and again instils an 'allegorical' character such as we find in the *Nativity* and *Crucifixion* of the Isenheim altarpiece. Actually the two saints were contemporaries about A.D. 300: but Erasmus was bishop of Antioch and suffered martyrdom under Diocletian, Maurice was a Roman officer and was sent from Africa with his Theban legion to suppress a Christian uprising in Gaul. On his way there he was himself converted to Christianity by bishop Sabas of Jerusalem, and was executed together with his troops in the Rhône valley.

The inner significance attaching to the meeting has not yet been fully explained. Erasmus is accompanied by a cleric. Maurice has a military escort. Is it a conversion scene, or the welcoming of the new patron Erasmus by the old one, Maurice? It is more probable that it represents a religious disputation. Not only gestures and expressions but also the attributes of the persons in question point to the problem involved here. The protagonists regard one another seriously, almost aggressively; their gestures are vehement, even those of Erasmus who plants his staff almost defensively between the armour-plated legs of the Moor. The attributes of Erasmus-Albrecht are the instruments of the pious man's martyrdom and the peaceful, pastoral staff. Maurice's attributes, on the other hand, are the sword and armour of the knight, the crown of the mighty. Forebearance in the face of attack: it is known that the liberal-minded cardinal who, with Erasmus of Rotterdam in mind, here identifies himself with the latter's holy namesake, carefully weighed both attitudes towards the advancing Reformation. To begin with he decided on toleration and in 1521 wrote conciliatory, almost humble letters to Luther. Not until 1525 did he become the fanatical opponent of the Reformation. In the Maurice-disputation as depicted by Grünewald, he is still the man who desires tolerance and peace

to prevail over open war – expressed in his own words: 'Let us not conduct our defence with threats and insults, not with arms and injustice, but with simple understanding, goodwill and mutual trust (Grote, *Erasmus-Mauritiustafel*, Stuttgart 1957, 17). The *Disputation* panel is one of a number of related works. A wood engraving by Hans Lemberger in a missal printed in Leipzig 1522, opens the series (E. Tiezte-Conrat, *Mitt. d. Gesellschaft für vervielfält. Künste*, Vienna 1927, 36 ff.). The most important parallel for the painting is provided by the sculptured group of the same saints, one of the series of monumental pillar figures in the church for which Grünewald had produced his altar panel: the collegiate church of Halle. The date of completion of this series of statues is 1525; the sculptured variant was thus in all probability done, under Grünewald's influence, immediately after the painted ones. Whereas the Erasmus and Maurice statues are close to the painted Disputation picture, individual features in the reliquary busts of the same saints and in the large silver figure of St. Maurice, for which Grünewald's influence is no less to be assumed, correspond down to the last detail both with the sculptured and the painted versions: St. Maurice e.g. wears the pearl headdress that he wears in Grünewald's painting while the same Annunciation can be seen on St. Erasmus's mitre as on the sculptured work by Ludwig Binder, etc. (The treasures of the 'Halle Heiltum', lost but for a few pieces, are known to us from the illustrations in two catalogues: one of 1520 (with wood engravings) and one of 1525 (with excellent miniatures; in the Aschaffenburg abbey library; facsimile publication by Halm-Berliner, Berlin 1931).

IX: Plates 76–80

SO-CALLED TAUBERBISCHOFS-HEIM ALTARPIECE

Karlsruhe, Kunsthalle.

Crucifixion and The Carrying of the Cross. Pinewood, each 77×60 in. (195.5×152.5 cm.), front and back of a panel.

The origin of the panel cannot be traced further back than the XVIII century. Actually, however, the trail leads considerably further.

The execution which is characteristic for Grünewald's latest style has always, on stylistic grounds, been dated around 1525, the date of the great rising which in 1526 allegedly cost Grünewald his position as court painter. It is possible that the panel, perhaps completed in Frankfurt, was for that reason never delivered. At any rate in 1526/27 when Grünewald was staying at Frankfurt he had with him a large picture that could not be stowed in a case when he left, which according to Zülch (1938, 375) was described as follows in the inventory of his estate: '2 lid an eyn taffel sin wiss bereidt und uff dem einen i crucifix, Maria und Sant Johannes' (the passage is obscure, it refers to two sides of a panel on one of which is a Crucifix with the Virgin and St. John but the words 'wiss bereidt' are incomprehensible). Zülch, too, was puzzled as to the meaning of the passage and suggested for 'wiss' the word 'aus' (out): 'aus bereidt' would then have to be understood as 'auch aussen bemalt' (also painted on the outside). The description: a Crucifix between the Virgin and St. John can in any case refer only to one picture by Grünewald: The *Crucifixion* on the severed Karlsruhe panel. No other Passion panel by Grünewald exists consisting of these three figures so that nothing is more likely than that the document should refer to a work which on every other count belongs to the particular period referred to in the inventory of 1528, namely about 1526.

In 1528 the panel painted on both sides was in the house of the silk embroiderer Hans of Saarbrücken in Frankfurt. After a lawsuit in 1539 the whole of Grünewald's estate went to his adopted son Andreas Nithardt, who was a teacher in Frankfurt in 1553.

At the beginning of the XVIII century, the panel – placed on a pivot – was on the Holy Cross altar of the parish church of Tauberbischofsheim, where the vicar, J. S. Severus, admired the 'elegans pictura artificis Alberti Dureri manufacta' (Zülch 1938, 330). In 1873 the German painter Hans Thoma was profoundly impressed by the panel and drew the attention of Eisenmann, director of the Kassel gallery, to it who in 1877 identified it as a work by Grünewald. In 1888 J.-K. Huysmans saw it in the Kassel museum. In 1889 the panel returned to Tauberbischofsheim and in 1899 was purchased by the Karlsruhe Kunsthalle under Hans Thoma, the director at the time.

The question as to whether the Karlsruhe panels formed part of a monumental altarpiece of the Passion the other parts of which are lost, or whether only a single panel was intended, has been convincingly answered by H. A. Schmid in the latter sense.

In 1883 the panel was cut apart (after a restoration of the back had revealed the *Carrying of the Cross* previously covered over) and split into two pictures. In 1900 a new restoration took place at Karlsruhe. According to H. A. Schmid (1911, 232) the panels have not been cut down at the edges; the condition of the paintings is certainly not unimpaired even though we must bear in mind that in these very large-size pictures, his latest ones, Grünewald paid little attention to careful execution, to an even distribution of the paint and to purity of colour. Certain passages are handled with great freedom and spontaneity; we gain the impression that Grünewald himself added paint thickly to some parts without previously removing all the layers beneath down to the primed surface with the drawing. Such indifference to the technical side is only paralleled in the *Dead Christ* in Aschaffenburg.

With reference to the inscription on the architectural frieze on the *Carrying of the Cross*: ESAIAS. 53. ER . IST . VMB . VNSER . SVND . WILLEN . GESCLAGEN (He was beaten for our sins), Zülch (1938, 262) notes that Grünewald must have taken this German text from a Passion Play since 'the Lutheran translation was not available at that time'. Passion plays, because they were vividly staged, probably were often the true source for realistic renderings of the Passion.

In its quiet symmetry the Karlsruhe *Crucifixion* is the most classic of Grünewald's paintings. For this, his unequivocal 'Renaissance work', he had adopted a type of Crucifixion the exemplary, widely influential Renaissance character of which had been established in Upper Italy, especially Venice, Ferrara and Bologna, during the second half of the quattrocento.

ATTRIBUTION (not illustrated)

Paintings from the Lindenhardt altarpiece.

Backs of the wings, representing the 14 Holy Helpers, $62\frac{5}{8} \times 27$ in. (159 × 68.5 cm.) each.

On the back of the shrine a standing figure, *Man of Sorrows*, $66\frac{1}{2} \times 60\frac{1}{4}$ in. (169 × 153 cm.).

Lindenhardt near Bayreuth, Parish Church.

On the outside of the shrine on the left is the date 1503. The altarpiece was transferred from Bindlach to its present place in 1685. Its original destination is unknown, but this must have been in the diocese of Bamberg which included the parish church of Bindlach. Represented among the carved figures of the right wing, namely, are the Emperor Henry and Empress Kunigunde the patron saints of Bamberg (Zülch, 1938, 81 ff., 323). It is, however, interesting to note that in the Badische Kunsthalle, Karlsruhe, there is a panel with *Seven Holy Helpers*, which is obviously connected in theme with the Lindenhardt altarpiece and is there described as from Augsburg (School of Hans Burgkmair).

The figures on the left wing represent SS. Margaret, Catherine, Barbara, George, Christopher, Pantaleon, Eustace; those on the right wing: Egidius, Cyriac, Achatius, Dionysius, Erasmus, Vitus.

The paintings of the Lindenhardt altarpiece were first claimed for Grünewald by K. Sitzmann (*Die Lindenhardter Altarflügel*, Bayreuth 1926). There can be no doubt that very close relations to Grünewald do exist, particularly in the heads and hands of the men. The decisive obstacle to accepting his authorship, however, lies in the date of origin – 1503, since the same date has been definitely established for the unquestionably authentic *Mocking of Christ* in Munich, which is incomparably finer in artistic quality and deviates considerably from the Lindenhardt panels in style. In spite of the repeated restorations (1685, 1897; cf. Zülch 1938, 81, 323) and the decomposition of the colours it is easy to see from the linear pattern with its mannerist wealth of curves, from the schematic drapery, the monotonous colours, the lack of originality in the composition and the generally vacant expressions, that Grünewald could never have painted the Lindenhardt altarpiece at the same time that he painted the Munich *Mocking of Christ*. The former might conceivably be regarded as a successful workshop production (as does Vogt 1957, 33). Zülch suggested a 'copy after Grünewald' (1938, 81, 323): as the conjectural author of the sculpture he thinks of Grünewald's friend, the Seligenstadt carver Arnold Rücker.